What People Are Saying about Sheer Commitment

The threat against marriage today is very real. In the secular world, there are more people who are cohabitating than ever before, and the numbers are rising. What is really disturbing is that a recent Barna statistic stated that born-again Christians are just as likely to divorce as non-Christians.

I don't know about you, but it seems to me that nobody wants to make commitments anymore. We don't want to commit to the gym we pay money to, nor to our church community that we pledged our faithfulness to as a believer, and now, regrettably, to our marriages. But there is encouragement coming from Stacey Gay and her book, *Sheer Commitment*!

This is a story, but not only a story; this is a testimony of how *sheer commitment,* dedication, and God-gumption can save your marriage, your family, and your legacy. Listen to this well-seasoned minister of the Gospel, beloved wife, mother, treasured grandmother, and dedicated carrier of the flame for marriages. Learn from her own hard experiences and glean from her devotion to her Heavenly Father as she trod out the steps of a successful and thriving relationship with her husband, Pastor Robert Gay, through many decades. Read these pages well, for in them, you will find the wellsprings of love and life.—**Pastor Judy Jacobs,** Psalmist/Author, Dwelling Place Church International, Chattanooga, TN

Stacey Gay is a prominent prophetic voice in our generation who has demonstrated her strong commitment to marriage and family. Throughout this book, Stacey shares personal experiences from her past, along with fresh insights from the Holy Spirit, designed to guide couples toward lasting relationships. *Sheer Commitment* is a valuable resource for pastors who offer premarital counseling and for long-term couples seeking to rekindle their commitment to one another. I highly recommend this book.—**Pastor Christa Meckfessel**, The Ridge Assembly, Little Rock, AR

Sheer Commitment—we love the title of this book. Stacey Gay's devotion to marriage and family not only shines through her writing, but it beams with the light of devotion to the Lord Himself. We know the Gays personally, and they practice what they preach. Their marriage and the children they have produced are a testament that doing life God's way works! This book will accomplish the same thing for you—a further walk and greater flow of moving with Him in excellence and accuracy concerning your marriage and family. May you learn to walk with Him in *sheer commitment*.—**Pastor Ken & Trudi Blount,** Ken Blount Ministries (KBM), Oklahoma City, OK

I highly recommend *Sheer Commitment*. An incredible book on commitment and marriage. With wisdom and authenticity, Stacey Gay offers valuable insights into building trust, navigating challenges, and deepening love. Whether you are in a new relationship or a long-term marriage, this book is a thoughtful, inspiring read that will resonate with anyone looking to strengthen their marital bond.—**Lindsey Doss**, Author, Hamilton, AL

STACEY GAY

MARRIAGE
& THE THINGS
WE ***DON'T***
TALK ABOUT

SHEER COMMITMENT

foreword by **JANE HAMON**

Melbourne, Florida
Published and Printed in the USA.

Sheer Commitment—Marriage & the Things We Don't Talk About
by Stacey Gay

With a Foreword by Pastor Jane Hamon.

Parsons Publishing House
P. O. Box 410063
Melbourne, FL 32940 USA
Info@ParsonsPublishingHouse.com

Publisher has opted to reference satan and related names with lowercase letters.

Cover Art by Micah Gay.
Cover art photo by Kelly Creamer Photography.

ISBN-13: 978-160273-163-9
ISBN-10: 160273163-2
Library of Congress Number: 2025935360
Printed in the United States of America.
For World-Wide Distribution.

Dedication

To my beloved husband, Robert Gay.

For forty-four years, you have been my rock, my greatest blessing, and my truest love. Your unwavering faith, impeccable character, and steadfast devotion have shaped my life and the lives of our three children and nine precious grandchildren. You have led our family with wisdom, grace, and a heart fully surrendered to the voice of the Holy Spirit, showing us what it means to walk in faith, integrity, and love.

Beyond our home, God has allowed us to minister together, impacting countless lives through the calling He placed on us. From the pulpit to personal moments of counsel and prayer, we have walked hand-in-hand, pouring His truth and love into the hearts of those He entrusted to our care. What an honor it has been to serve alongside you, to see lives transformed, and to witness God's faithfulness in every season!

I loved you when I was young, and I will love you when I am old. I will love you in the good times and even when life is difficult. My love for you will remain steadfast. I promise to love you forever.

With all my heart,
Stacey

SHEER COMMITMENT

TABLE OF CONTENTS

PREFACE

by Pastor Robert Gay

Many years ago, my wife, Stacey Gay, was encouraged by numerous people to author a book on marriage. I was also one of those prodding her to do so. She began to question, "Why write a book when there are already wonderful ones written on marriage—and who would want to read what I have to say?" That is a legitimate question that needed an answer in her mind. Of course, I immediately told her there were people everywhere who needed to hear her insight and wisdom. The good news is that she got her answer and has now written this masterful book, ***Sheer Commitment.***

Everyone has life experiences that are unique and different. Throughout our journey, there are things that we learn and assimilate. While certain core biblical principles always remain constant, the applications of these truths are different and varied with every individual. Throughout our forty years of marriage, we have experienced many things that were distinctive to us. Every step along the way, we learned things that helped strengthen both our faith and marriage.

I can personally attest to the authenticity and depth of the insights contained in this book. When I first read Stacey's writing, tears came to my eyes as the "realness" of her words touched my heart. In a world of books that are often clinical in their approach, this was so refreshing. Her book is a heartfelt testament to her journey through life's challenges and triumphs, and she shares her experiences with a level of transparency that is both needed and inspiring.

Stacey takes readers on a journey through the intricate tapestry of marital life, weaving in her own stories and lessons learned over decades. Her transparency allows readers to see the real struggles and joys that come with marriage. She does not shy away from sharing the difficult moments, which makes her insights all the more relatable. This heartfelt approach invites readers to reflect on their own experiences and encourages them to engage with the content on a personal level.

What sets this book apart is its practical nature. Stacey takes timeless biblical principles and translates them into actionable steps that couples can easily incorporate into their daily lives. She emphasizes that a strong marriage is not just a matter of luck; it requires intentionality, effort, and yes, ***sheer commitment***. Each chapter is filled with practical applications that can empower couples to strengthen their relationships, whether they are newlyweds or have been together for decades.

Throughout the years, I had the privilege of witnessing Stacey's teachings come to life in our own marriage. I have seen her practice what she preaches, from fostering open communication to prioritizing quality time together. Her wisdom is not just theoretical; it is grounded in real-life experiences that she has navigated with grace and resilience. The practical strategies she offers have strengthened our marriage and can undoubtedly do the same for others.

Stacey's book encourages readers to embrace vulnerability, communicate openly, and build a foundation of trust and respect. She provides tools for conflict resolution and emphasizes the importance of forgiveness while reminding readers that every relationship will face challenges and how we respond to them can make all the difference. By sharing her own stories, she illustrates how these principles can lead to a deeper connection and a more fulfilling partnership.

In a world where the institution of marriage is often challenged, Stacey's insights serve as a guiding light for couples seeking to strengthen their bonds. Her heartfelt narrative, combined with practical applications, makes this book a valuable resource for anyone looking to enhance their marriage. It is not just a guide; it is an invitation to embark on a journey of growth, understanding, and love.

I highly recommend this masterpiece, ***Sheer Commitment.*** Stacey's transparent storytelling, insightful teachings, and practical applications make it a must-read for couples at any stage of their relationship. It is a beautiful reminder that with dedication, faith, and the right tools, marriages can thrive and flourish, just as ours has for over forty years. ***Sheer Commitment*** is more than a title for a book, it is the criterion for a successful marriage and family!

Pastor Robert Gay, Panama City, FL USA
High Praise Ministerial Alliance, Author/songwriter, devoted husband, father, and grandfather

SHEER COMMITMENT

FOREWORD

by Pastor Jane Hamon

When I was sixteen years old, the Lord spoke to me in an audible voice and instructed me to go to Bible College rather than the secular school where I had a scholarship. Part of what God said was that when I got there, I would meet a man. When my husband, Tom, hears me tell this story, he always adds the words "a handsome, anointed man." Ha! The Lord said we would get married young and be thrust into the ministry. We would travel to the nations of the earth. Sometimes, he would preach, and sometimes, I would preach because He was making us a ministry team. This was back in the late 70s, and I had never seen a husband and wife ministry team before, so I asked the Lord to show me someone who was doing what I would be doing. He responded with these words, "There is no one doing now what you will be doing then, for I will be doing a new thing."

I did indeed go off to Bible College and met my husband, Tom, my first night on campus. We fell madly in love right from the beginning. We were engaged within the year and married within two. We planted our first church two months after we were married and our second church by our mid-twenties, which we are still pastoring almost forty years later. At this writing, we have traveled to sixty-seven nations as a team. Sometimes, he preaches, and sometimes, I preach. We are joyfully fulfilling what God intended for our lives.

Some might say we were a match made in heaven. While marriages may be made in heaven, so is thunder and lightning! Think about that! Though we have served the Lord our whole marriage, life has not always been easy. We have had to grow together through unexpected challenges: multiple miscarriages, a son born needing over thirteen corrective surgeries, times of poverty and lack, a special needs grandson, challenges in our health, and yes, times of stress and disagreement. We have walked through the heartbreak of lost friendships due to ministerial differences, challenges in relating to extended family, many of whom we are blessed to work with, and the pressures that come with raising a family and living our lives as public figures and all the demands put on us.

How have we managed to navigate all of life's challenges and remain strong and in love all these years later? ***Sheer Commitment***. I love the name of this book written by Stacey Gay. It so encapsulates how husbands and wives keep their love young and alive and grow stronger with each passing year. Let me explain:

In today's culture, marriage relationships go through these five stages:

First, there is a connection. This is when you click. You are attracted to one another, and it seems as if the other person can do nothing wrong. You have stars in your eyes and see the other person as almost perfect, or at least perfect for you. This is the spark that starts everything.

The second is commitment. You are so in love that you commit to love the other person in good times and bad, in sickness and in health, 'til death do us part. It usually involves a glorious day of celebration, and you feel on top of the world, ready to take on any challenge.

Thirdly, you find yourself in a place of conflict. Suddenly, the honeymoon is over, and you are faced with your partner's imperfections. Previously you believed you were so alike. Now you realize you couldn't be more different. This is the stage where you may experience anger, frustration, or resentment toward your spouse and all the challenges that come with those emotions. It can be a very trying time.

Fourth is the important make-or-break stage called choices. This is where the rubber meets the road. Will you choose to love, forgive, and walk through conflict, finding a solution to your differences by listening to one another and to the Lord for help? Or will you choose to withdraw from one another, live in anger, hurt each other, and ultimately break your relationship through divorce? If you choose to do things God's way, you can move into stage five.

Fifth is living in a place of deep covenant with one another. This is the stage of living in forever-love. This is the walking out and working out of "'til death do us part." This is the place of ceasing to change the other person to be like you but rather learning to celebrate your differences and be strengthened by them. This is the place for learning what it means to live as a team, even if your callings and responsibilities are different from one another. Every good team has players with different gifts and skillsets. This is the stage of deep, abiding love and desire that will sustain your marriage beyond the first spark into a slow-burning fire that will warm you throughout your lives together.

So, while marriages may be made in heaven, they are lived here on this earth, with the good, the bad, and, at times, the ugly. This is why I am so grateful that Stacey Gay has taken the time to write ***Sheer Commitment***. I love that she is vulnerable and, at times, raw about the challenges in her own marriage and how she and Robert walked through times of conflict into a deep place of covenant forever-love. Tom and I have walked together for almost forty years with Robert and Stacey Gay. As a matter of fact, we were married in the same year, one day apart. (They have us beat by a day!). We have watched them grow and love and grow some more, just as they have watched us navigate our own challenges.

This book will help you grow in your marriage and the principles will enhance every relationship you have. As you read, you may laugh or cry, but you will definitely gain a deeper understanding of attaining a Christ-centered, victorious marriage that will last a lifetime. You will discover the truth that this kind of love doesn't always come easily, but when you practice ***sheer commitment*** to the Lord and to one another, you can experience heaven on earth no matter what you face.

Thank you, Stacey, for this treasure. May it bring life to marriages everywhere.

Pastor Jane Hamon, Santa Rosa Beach, FL USA
Co-pastor Vision Church @ Christian International

Introduction

by Kayla Hill

I am writing with great enthusiasm to recommend ***Sheer Commitment***, a powerful and insightful book by my mother, Stacey Gay. Having had the privilege of growing up in her home, I have witnessed firsthand the principles she so beautifully articulates in this book. She has lived the truths she writes about, and the lessons within these pages have shaped my understanding of what it means to build a marriage and family based on biblical values.

Over the years, I have seen my mother's unwavering dedication to build a strong, godly marriage with my father. Her commitment has never been superficial but rather rooted in deep, heartfelt devotion to God, her husband, and our family. As a wife and mother, she has always strived to be a living example of the biblical roles and responsibilities described in Scripture. Whether it was in moments of joy or in times of trial, her faithfulness never wavered. Her example has been a guiding light for me and many others, showing that a strong marriage is not merely a product of love and compatibility but of dedication, sacrifice, and a commitment to God's Word.

Sheer Commitment offers practical wisdom and sound advice for women who are seeking to strengthen their marriages and embrace the roles of wife and mother with grace and purpose. It provides a solid foundation for building a marriage that is not only enduring but thriving, with the Word of God as its cornerstone. My mother's wisdom and authenticity shine through every page, and I have no doubt that this book will be an invaluable resource for anyone looking to create a lasting, godly marriage.

Whether you are newly married or have been walking in marriage for many years, this book will offer you the tools you need to nurture a relationship that reflects God's design for marriage. I wholeheartedly believe in the message of ***Sheer Commitment***, and I know it will help countless couples build marriages that stand the test of time.

Kayla Hill, Daughter, Orlando FL USA

1
WHAT DID YOU SAY?

Many years ago, my husband, Robert, and I were shopping at our local mall. As we were walking and conversing with one another, we ran into an old friend. We greeted one another and exchanged pleasantries. We shared about our family and how our children were doing. It was a delight to reconnect after not seeing them for several years.

During our conversation, the subject of our thirtieth wedding anniversary came up. Our friend asked my husband, "What is the secret to the longevity of your marriage?" I expected he would respond with an extremely sweet and sentimental answer. Being married that long would be worthy of a romantic and meaningful response.

Without blinking an eye, he boldly said these words, "***Sheer commitment***!" I was surprised and shocked, to say the least. Where were the words, "*I'm madly in love with her*"? Where was the statement, "*She takes my breath away*"? Why did he not say, "*I can't imagine life without her*"? He did not mention any of these things; his reply was simply, "***Sheer commitment.***"

Shocked and Surprised

I quickly, and perhaps not so politely, squeezed his arm and looked at him in disbelief because his response somewhat hurt me. I was shocked when he replied with that choice of words. It was offensive to me that there were no flowery words of deep love and adoration. My expectation was that he would express his passionate feelings for the relationship we shared for all those years. However, none of that happened, and he did not respond as I expected.

Truthfully, I felt his response was unfeeling toward me. At that moment, I did not want to hear the words, "***Sheer commitment.***" I wanted words of love and acceptance to be communicated. In my mind, the words "***sheer commitment***" were him simply stating that he had no other option. He was stuck! I was the proverbial old ball and chain!

I am certain that through my expressions of displeasure, he understood that I was not happy with his response. He quickly began to explain his choice for using the words "***sheer commitment.***" He explained that commitment is required to be successful at anything in life. I then understood his actual statement declared he was, without reservation, totally committed to me, our family, and our life together. The way I initially perceived his statement was not his actual intent.

As I listened, it made so much sense and made me reflect on our married years. I began to think about the good times and the not-so-good times. I recalled the most amazing times and the downright tough times. It was a bell-ringing moment as I recognized that the entire reason we were still married was solely because we were committed to each other—not because of a romantic feeling we had on our wedding day or any day since then. It really was "***sheer commitment.***"

Wedding Day vs. Married Life

It seems that in today's world, we want everything to be easy, fast, and personally rewarding. However, this is not marriage; it is a fairy tale. It is like the fantasy that so many young girls have of Prince Charming whisking them away on his white horse to take them to his castle, where problems never exist. Unfortunately, this is not the reality in which any of us live, even when we find our Prince Charming. The choice to have a "Happy Ever After" is decided by us and the commitment we make to the relationship.

Many people today are in love with the idea of the wedding day, but they fail to give much thought to what is needed for the "Happy Ever After." They spend so much time and money planning and preparing for the big event rather than their married life. They invest thought and emotion into that one wedding day, and give little to no time considering the days, months, and years to follow. We must understand that marriage is a commitment encompassing a lifetime, not a single day.

We exchange vows on our wedding day, promising to love in the good times and the not-so-good times, in the lean seasons and the seasons of plenty, in sickness and health, and for better or worse. It is a sad thought, but many people never live up to those vows. At the first sign of adversity, they want to pack up and move on. The vows are quickly forgotten because they were only words said on their beautiful day when all the attention was on them.

Unfortunately, most people do not consider or put any thought into the meaning and weightiness of those spoken words. As soon as adversity and challenges arise (and they do), vows are forgotten, promises are broken, and many people give up on their marriage. This behavior eventually leads them down the road of separation or divorce. We must understand that the times of adversity are when we need each other the most. That is when "***sheer commitment***" must be enacted and displayed.

It is easy to love and be committed to someone when everything is coming up roses. It is easy with ample money in the bank and no financial problems. It is easy when your spouse agrees with you, and there are no conflicting opinions. However, that is not our everyday reality.

Fairy Tale or Real Life?

We do not live in a Snow White world full of knights with shining armor riding in to rescue us from every problem. Marriage does not guarantee that you will wake up each morning with a kiss and then be serenaded by your spouse at the end of every day with a beautiful sunset as your backdrop. A successful relationship requires being committed to one another at every moment in every season. It encompasses total heart dedication to each other and overcoming life's challenges together.

So many people today pattern their marriages after Hollywood movies, romance novels, or even their best friend's marital relationship. It is paramount to understand that every marriage has unique characteristics, and every individual has unique personality traits. Each marriage will be different. The way that you relate to your spouse is not necessarily the same as another couple. Refrain from comparing your relationship to others.

Recognize that you are unique and created to complement your spouse. As a couple, you were created to complete each other, not compete with one another. You each bring something special to the relationship that should be celebrated, not criticized. I am glad my husband and I do not have the same strengths and weaknesses. He is everything I need, and I am everything he needs. We are incomplete without each other. When this simple thought and understanding crystallizes in your heart and mind, you will stop competing and begin to experience a marriage where strife is no longer present.

Having been married for over forty years, my husband, Robert, and I have been through an array of things, some good and some not-so-wonderful. We are not superhuman or exempt from life's challenges just because we are in the ministry. We have not been given any special superpower, grace, or love that is not available to every believer. We are still together today because of one primary thing: the choice to stay committed to each other through it all.

What's the Secret?

My husband correctly answered when he replied to the question asked, "What's the secret to the longevity of your marriage?" ***Sheer commitment*** is the only way to succeed in your marriage and home. It requires total and 100% commitment! It requires you to be "all in," holding back nothing. This is the principle by which your marriage will succeed and become everything you dreamed it to be. This is truly the way to your "Happily Ever After" and being together forever.

In this book, I want to give you an encapsulation of things we have learned, experienced, and lived out! You may laugh, you may cry, and you may even be shocked! Through my own real-life stories coupled with biblical principles, it is my desire to help equip you to have a beautiful, successful, and "Happily Ever After" kind of marriage—one that will last like our traditional marriage vows state, "Until death do us part."

Feelings and emotions can be fluid and fleeting, but a decision to be committed will carry you through the difficult moments and trials of life. ***Sheer commitment*** to one another will cause you to withstand every storm and see victory in your personal life, marriage, and family.

Ask Yourself

Take a look inside and ponder for a moment. Were you more excited about your wedding day or the person to whom you are married today? Did the ceremony experience mean more to you then than your spouse does now? Are you fully committed for the long haul, or was it merely a moment of emotion you now regret? These are questions only you can answer but will determine the success of your marriage. Let ***sheer commitment*** be your answer. I promise it will work for you just like it did for my husband and me.

2

The Clarinet, The Cutie, The Commitment

As a little girl, I recall wanting to be like my mother. She married young and had given birth to me and my three siblings before she was twenty-three years old. When she showed up at school events, I had a sense of pride because she was so beautiful and young, which seemed uncommon compared to all my friends' parents. I used to tell my mother that I wanted to grow up and be a "wife and mommy" just like her. She was a stay-at-home mom, and I loved how she was always present and available to us. I wanted to be like that for my future husband and children.

She made everything look so easy, and I wanted that simple, carefree life. Now, I laugh about saying that since I fully understand all the work involved in being a stay-at-home mom. I have personally experienced the daily sacrifices necessary to create a loving home that is a fun and safe place to live. It is extremely hard work.

As a family, we watched the Lawrence Welk show together, and I wanted to play the clarinet like the man I often watched on the show. His musical ability was intriguing, and I thought learning to play would be easy and fun. In junior high school,

I had the opportunity to be in the band and decided to join, having no understanding of the work, commitment, and practice needed to be a great clarinet player. I thought I would just pick it up and play like the man on the television show in no time. I found out quickly that my ideas were not reality. However, something lasting did come from my desire to play the clarinet, even though I never achieved my goal of being a great clarinetist.

The Band Assistant

Little did I know that the beginning band class had several student assistants tasked with helping new students like me. One of those assistants was a good-looking young teenage boy named Robert Gay, the first-chair trumpet player in the Advanced Band. The moment I saw him, I knew he was my Prince Charming. Yes, I knew this had to be love. It was then that I understood the meaning of "love at first sight." He was so cute, and my crush was so big that I was unable to play my clarinet in front of him, which presented a big problem.

How was this a problem? Each week, we were required to "pass off" or successfully play our technique lessons for the student assistants. I was an immature seventh grader with a huge crush on Robert, who determined where each person ranked in the section; therefore, I could only laugh, squeak, and squawk on my clarinet while attempting this routine task. He was first in my heart, but because of my crush on him and the fact that he was not impressed with my musical abilities, I often sat in the last chair.

Robert did not even know I existed. I was just a silly, immature, unaccomplished "wanna-be" clarinet player. On the other hand, he was a ninth grader who was voted most talented in the school, and the faculty of Everett Junior High awarded him the "Mr. Everett" title. He was focused and serious about school and band. But again, in my immaturity, I told my last-chair clarinet friend, "I'm going to marry him one day." I said that when I was in the seventh grade. I am not sure if I was speaking prophetically or just a young girl dreaming.

Divine Detour

Upon completion of the school year, Robert moved on to high school while I still had two years left in junior high. I was unsure if I would ever see him again, but to my surprise, his family began to attend the Assembly of God church where my family and I were members. My hopes were sparked once again. I was thrilled and excited because I had not given up on the hope that my seventh-grade dream could still become a reality one day.

By the end of my ninth-grade year, Robert and I had become friends and started speaking frequently—or flirting—with each other. High school band rehearsals and tryouts began, and Robert would drive me and his younger brother to the high school for tryouts and practice every afternoon. It appeared that he had noticed me, finally, after three long years!

When I began my sophomore year of high school, I was excited to attend the same school as Robert. As the school year began, I was thrilled that we were scheduled to have some classes together. However, he had chosen to participate in a prototype program and attend college his senior year. My heart sank. How were we going to be able to see each other? How would my dream be fulfilled if we could not be together?

Several months later, he asked if he could pick me up from a church hayride in October 1978. We talked on the car ride home, and he walked me to my door. That was the start of our ongoing relationship. Soon after, he became my boyfriend, and I was his girlfriend. Years later, he asked me to marry him, and we were engaged on Christmas Day of my senior year. We were married 11 days after I graduated on June 12th, 1981.

My Dream Became a Reality

My dream came true, but our lives were just starting. My dream became a living reality; it manifested in my life, and it was real. However, my dreams omitted all the challenges we would later face. The day that my dream was fulfilled was when the real work began.

I fell in love years before our wedding, but after we were married, I had to make a choice to love. REAL is always different than what you dream. REAL can be hard! REAL can hurt at times! REAL is not always butterflies and bubbles. REAL means changes and challenges. Dreams can become REAL, but REAL involves work and persistence. REAL requires commitment; it demands that we choose to love, which calls for sacrifice.

The fact is that feelings and emotions change, but commitment is a daily choice—committing to believe the best, be your best, and love even if you are mad, sad, or hurt. For any relationship to survive and thrive, both parties must choose to be true to the vows promised. Be a person of your word, even if your flesh is screaming otherwise. Love is not a feeling but an action.

Beautiful Diamonds Go Through a Process

Today, I treasure the reality I have far more than the fairy tale dream I had as a little girl. Even though that reality required a process, it was worth it. Diamonds are not naturally beautiful; they are formed under extreme pressure and high temperatures. Ultimately, they undergo a process to bring out the beauty and values they truly possess. When first discovered, they are dull and extremely lackluster. They must go through a transformation to become beautiful and desirable. The value of the diamond is already present, but without the process, no one can see or appreciate it. Likewise, every person, every couple, every relationship, and every marriage must go through a process to become beautiful. You must look beyond the ugly, hard, and dull to see the hidden value. We must allow the Holy Spirit to unveil the beauty and worth that was there all along.

I am thankful for the process that God took Robert and me through to become who we are today. Even though there were times of pain and discomfort, the fruit of yielding our lives and relationship to the Lord has resulted in a beautiful marriage. Placing Him first and allowing Him to mold us caused the blossoming of something greater than I imagined when I was a young girl. Our relationship became more than I ever dreamed!

God Is Committed to Us

Think for a moment about the attributes of God. There are so many wonderful things that can be articulated concerning Him. However, since we are talking about commitment, no one is more committed to us than the Lord. He was so committed that He sent Jesus, His only Son, to suffer and die, even when we did not deserve it. That is the ultimate ***sheer commitment***!

Jesus did not say upon arrival to earth, "*These people aren't worth it; they hurt me, so I'm canceling the contract.*" He never said, "*I am better off without them.*" NO! Jesus fulfilled the plan and purpose set before Him and kept His promise. He did not quit when people cursed, betrayed, and mocked him; He simply forgave them and remembered His commitment to fulfill His assignment. He continued to love regardless of what He encountered.

Likewise, since we are made in His image and likeness, we should honor our commitments. We should imitate the Lord and be faithful to our promises, and it should begin with our marriages, considering it is the most important earthly contract of all. It is the commitment of all commitments!

We Need Each Other!

It is so easy in today's culture to become self-reliant and embrace an attitude that you can do it all by yourself. However, that is not God's plan for you, nor will it ever be. God said it is not good for man to be alone. This was settled at the beginning of creation when Adam and Eve were created. Similarly, we need to firmly establish this principle within our own hearts.

The fundamental truth that should be understood within the heart of every man and woman is that we need each other! God created you for someone, and likewise, He created someone for you! He gave Adam and Eve the commission to be fruitful, multiply, subdue, and take dominion! This was something they could only do together; it could not be done alone. They could not be fruitful and multiply without each other. The ability to fulfill God's commission to them was not present within the sole individual; rather, it required them to work together. Again, they needed one another just as we need each other today.

God did not say to Adam, "*Boy, you got this!*" On the contrary, he said that Adam needed someone to help him! With that thought, God took a rib from Adam's side and formed a woman. Man needed a woman; he needed someone to assist him. He needed a "help meet." Adam possessed a need that only Eve could fulfill, and he needed someone to complete him.

The words *help meet* mean "to stand out boldly opposite." God put two people together that were total opposites to fulfill his plan on earth. It is essential that we do not let our differences divide us. Moreover, we must realize that we all see from unique perspectives; while one person may hold one piece of the puzzle, the other may hold another. We need each other to fulfill the very plan and purpose of God. We should not view each other as adversaries but rather as those who complete one another.

The fact that people get married and need each other does not mean they live in a constant state of bliss. It does not mean there will never be conflicts or obstacles to overcome. Conversely, life brings with it an array of situations and struggles. Therefore, we must be committed to our marriage with Jesus at the center of it all.

Commitment Is Not a Dirty Word

Your marriage will only last if you commit to it. Unfortunately, it seems that commitment is a dirty word in the world today. It is sad to say that some people will curse before talking about commitment. It is one of those things we don't want to talk about. People do not want to be tied down, held accountable, or answer to anyone. While this seems prevalent in our current culture, we must understand that a marriage without commitment will not last. Without this quality, it cannot stand the test of time or the adversity that it will face.

Let us look for a minute at the meaning of the word commitment. It is simply defined as an agreement or pledge to do. We should never enter a marriage covenant without an understanding of commitment. No one should marry with the imaginary idea that it is the doorway to happiness and bliss, void of any challenges and obstacles. Instead, it should be embraced with the understanding that it is the doorway to a heart dedicated to work, and a pledge to do whatever is needed to be successful in your marriage.

Making a commitment involves giving yourself to someone completely. You must be "all in." You must have an "I do" and "I will" attitude! "I do" is not merely something you say at the altar during a wedding ceremony; it is equally a pledge that you choose to practice daily. It is something that requires action and effort every day that you live. It is a daily choice for a lifetime of living the dream together.

Some people have said that marriage is a 50/50 transactional contract. On the contrary, it is each person giving 100% of themselves twenty-four hours a day, seven days a week.

Marriages should never be transaction-based with the disposition, "*If you give, then I'll give.*" Instead, it is daily laying down your life as an unselfish sacrifice for each other. It is giving 100% from both the husband and wife every moment of every day! Any couple that is not giving in this manner will fail to experience the fullness of how beautiful a marriage relationship can be. It is essential that we do not withhold anything when it comes to giving to our spouse. Your marriage is worth all the sacrifice and work it takes to succeed.

Be the Right Person

Many years ago, as a young pastor, my husband was asked to perform a wedding ceremony for a couple in our church. Instead of using a ceremony written by someone else, he wrote his own. There are many things I love about his ceremony, but my favorite statement is one I believe should be said at EVERY wedding performed: "Marriages do not succeed based upon finding the right person, rather being the right person!" Let that sink in.

Are you always wanting your spouse to change or are you willing to look in the mirror and ask God to change you? This is something else that we don't want to talk about. The question is not if you found the right person but if you are willing to be the right person.

Being the right person puts responsibility on you. It does not point the finger at your husband or wife but at the person in the mirror. We should not place blame on our spouse for our feelings of unhappiness and misery, as is often done. Instead, we must take full responsibility for our feelings and be the best partner to our spouse that we can be.

If you are constantly unhappy, you may need to look introspectively and examine your own life and attitude. It is easy to deflect and blame your spouse when a face-to-face "come to Jesus meeting" with yourself is needed. You must take responsibility, adjust your feelings of ungratefulness, and choose to change any bad attitudes that are present. This will begin to bring about greater peace and joy, not only in your own life but also in the relationship with your spouse.

Ditch the List

Many people focus solely on finding the perfect person. They make their list of qualifications needed for their ideal spouse. Unfortunately, they create an unrealistic individual in their minds who does not exist. For a woman, it is their Prince Charming with flawless hair blowing in the wind and whose beautiful eyes pierce her soul. Add to that a perfectly fit body who is always the kindest gentleman, the greatest chef, the best future father, and has lots of money. For a man, he wants Miss America, who can cook, clean, have his babies, and look like a model walking down the runway while doing it all. However, most people waiting to find this imagined person will remain single until they choose to throw away their list. This is also something that we don't want to talk about. However, here we go!

Often, these lists include expectations of others that are unachievable by 99.99% of people. Ironically, the ones holding the lists cannot achieve the requirements either. They are searching for the perfect person while they are far beneath the standard they have set for the one in which they are in pursuit. They end up expecting perfection from the person they eventually marry while making excuses for their own shortcomings. The truth is if we focus our attention on being the right person, we will find the right person.

There are times I have heard people say, "*I think I married the wrong person.*" They feel that they are doomed to a miserable life and relationship because of the choice they made. However, their thinking and perspective are skewed because they lack the understanding that finding the right person is not the key to marital success; rather, it is being the right person. The issue is not finding the perfect individual; it is being the best spouse that you can be.

Before our children married, my husband and I told them that we would not tell them who they should marry as long as they were saved and serving the Lord. However, we did tell them this: "Once you say, 'I do,' you are done!" We reinforced to them that their marriage was not something entered into lightly and was a commitment for life. We instructed them that by the grace of God, any issue or challenge could be overcome if they kept Jesus at the center of their marriage.

Committed Means Submitted

When Robert and I were planning our wedding, we decided to write our own vows. I strongly despised the word *submit* and refused to use it in any of our vows, even though it is a biblical word. In my mind, it meant that I was giving up all rights to have an opinion or input into our lives or plans. I believed that subjugating my opinion to anyone else was equivalent to being controlled by them—and I was not going to have that at all.

The truth is that being submitted does not mean you subjugate yourself to control, abuse, and manipulation. It means that you trust God, your spouse, and your choice to enter a covenant together. Looking back, I wish I had possessed a greater understanding of the word and honored my husband by choosing to use the word in my vows to him. However, it did not change my commitment to him.

When we got married, I was young and did not have a full understanding of commitment or what marriage was meant to be. I would not allow myself to be vulnerable. I was always on guard and perceived any challenge as a personal attack. I did not understand that Robert and I were supposed to be a team. We each had a position and role, which is how any successful team works. The commitment to work together gives them the ability to win and succeed.

Through many trials and tears, I learned that submission is just another word for being committed. Refusing to submit was actually an expression of my failure to trust the team member I chose and my misunderstanding of the word. In essence, my refusal was a lack of faith in God, my future spouse, and marriage itself. This is another one of those things that we don't want to talk about. Yet here is the kicker: If we refuse to embrace biblical principles, we simultaneously reject God's help. Let that sink in for a moment. I had to repent.

Failure to follow God's design and commands for marriage is a manifestation of not believing God's Word. When we allow doubt to take control of our lives, we are refusing to do things God's way. Fear begins to control our thinking, and we fail to benefit from what He has ordained for us. We must recognize that when our marriages are modeled after God's design, we will experience His blessing, and our relationships will blossom and flourish. Refuse to allow fear to have control of your life and family.

Fully Committed

I am fully committed to my husband and God's plan for us. I am not afraid because I know that obedience to the Lord will always result in God's promises being fulfilled. I moved beyond the point of fear and embraced God's plan for our marriage. I moved beyond hoping my spouse would be the right person and chose to become the right person. Since then, God has fulfilled His promise within my life in a greater way than I ever imagined.

My relationship with Robert began when I joined band in the 7th grade. I dreamed of being a great clarinet player, but that dream failed to become a reality because I never fully committed to the required process. However, once we were married, I committed to our marriage relationship and that dream of becoming Robert's wife came true. The contrast is ironic but reveals the difference made by ***sheer commitment.*** Without it, there will undoubtedly be failure. Embrace commitment, and you will see success!

Sheer commitment is the only way to experience the kind of relationship that God intends for us to have as husbands and wives. Both partners must be fully committed and dedicated. There is no place for reservation or the withholding of a dedicated heart. It requires work and attentiveness to obey God's Word and follow His plan.

Commitment is what causes marriages to succeed today. It is not thrills and frills. It is not houses and cars. It is not two perfect spouses living in a perfect world. It sometimes comes down to the things we don't want to talk about. At the end of the day, it comes down to ***sheer commitment.***

Ask Yourself

Ask yourself: Do the words *committed* or *submitted* rub you the wrong way? Are you willing to be the right person rather than attempting to make your spouse the right person? Will you embrace the process of becoming the person your spouse needs rather than focusing on them meeting your needs? If you can answer these questions correctly, your marriage will be on the road to fulfillment. Otherwise, make the necessary adjustments so your marriage can be filled with joy and bliss.

3

It's More than a Feeling

I can still recall all the "mushy-gushy" feelings I felt as a young girl. I was infatuated with this boy and told my classmate in 7th grade about my plans to marry him. There were butterflies in my stomach every time I entered the room for him to evaluate my clarinet technique. I also clearly remember the feeling I had once he noticed me, and we began our relationship. Emotions of anticipation and excitement came alive for what possibly lay ahead for us as a couple. I felt joy and happiness when he talked to me. I was elated that the dream I had was finally happening. The boy I dreamed of was becoming a reality in my life.

As our relationship progressed, I remember our first kiss standing at the gate of my childhood home. Those feelings that every girl dreams of were just as I had expected. When Robert reached over to hold my hand, butterflies flooded my heart, and my emotions were stirred. I loved him; the feelings were strong, and I never wanted them to diminish. We were dating, and I was overjoyed! He was everything I ever hoped for: handsome, kind, attentive, and focused. He loved Jesus, and he loved me! He really was my Prince Charming.

The Promise and The Engagement

On July 4th, 1979, watching fireworks on the beach, Robert pulled a small box from his pocket. It was a very special birthday gift he had purchased for me. As I opened it, I was overcome with excitement and thrilled when my eyes saw a beautiful promise ring; I still have it to this day. Although the diamonds are so tiny that it takes a microscope to see them, I loved it because it was from him—my guy!

All the fireworks paled in comparison to that moment! My heart exploded as he placed it on my finger. It was his way of saying that he promised to be faithful to me until we could be engaged and married. It was truly special and brought so many emotions that I cried with joy. Again, all my dreams were becoming reality, and all the feelings of love continually grew stronger every day.

Since we started dating in my sophomore year of high school, it would be two years before we could even consider marriage, although we discussed it many times. Finally, Christmas of my senior year arrived, and he asked me to marry him! It was not a big production, but I didn't care. I found the one with whom I wanted to share my life forever. I did not need surprise roses or a blanket on the beach surrounded with candles in the shape of a heart, with a photographer hiding in the sea oats capturing "the moment." There is nothing wrong with these things, but our engagement looked a little different.

I was still in high school, and he was in college while helping with a church plant in our city. We did not have any money, but we loved each other. Regardless of what it took to be together, we were willing to make the sacrifices to make it happen.

The Pawn Shop

Robert's grandmother had remarried late in life, and she told us of a place where she and her husband had purchased their rings. It was a pawn shop called 50/50 Pawn Shop. Her rings were beautiful, and it sounded like a place we could afford. So, off we went with our small budget and found our entire wedding set for around $200, which included my engagement ring and both wedding rings. It was perfect, and I loved it! It was real! My little girl dreams and junior high crush were happening, and I was overjoyed. There was so much to look forward to, and the plans we had talked about for two years were in the process of becoming a reality.

I was so proud to show off my ring, and I did not care that it came from a pawn shop instead of Tiffany's®. For me, it was more than merely a ring on my finger; it represented the promise of my future with the love of my life that I had dreamed of for so many years. It embodied the dream I had possessed since I was in the 7th grade. With every passing day that drew us closer to that fulfillment, the feelings were accentuated and, at times, overwhelming! This love was a beautiful thing, and I could not wait to experience it for a lifetime.

Excitement and Anticipation

As our wedding day approached, the excitement grew! The thought of my 7th grade "crush" becoming my husband and partner in life was exciting. Most people look forward to high school prom, graduation, and all the graduation parties that follow, but not me! I wanted to skip graduation altogether, but we recognized it was necessary. So, I made it through to graduation night, knowing it was one event and one day closer to becoming Mrs. Robert Gay for the rest of my life.

Graduation day passed, and our wedding day was now only eleven days away. I was ready to say, "I do" and begin our life together. It was time to start a lifetime of love, bliss, and being together forever. Again, I could not contain the excitement and anticipation of what my "forever" held. I knew Robert was the one I had waited for my entire life. Everything was going to be perfect with the perfect man for me.

Wedding Day Arrives

In today's culture, weddings have become productions and huge expensive celebrations, but ours was not. Our wedding was beautiful, and my parents gave me everything I desired, which included nothing extravagant. My wedding dress was not a designer brand, but I loved it, nonetheless. The church was decorated with beautiful flowers, greenery, and candles that gave the perfect glow to the platform where our closest friends stood to witness our "big day." The church pews held our dearest friends and family, who attended the ceremony to witness the vows and commitment we made to one another.

It was a beautiful day, and I am thankful for it all. However, the one thing I cared the most about was that the man of my dreams was standing at the front of the church beside the minister who would pronounce us husband and wife. My dream would finally become reality. This was the day that started our forever together.

As you have deduced by now, we were not really prepared for the reality of marriage, but we knew we loved each other and were determined to make our relationship work. We were "young and dumb." We had no money for the honeymoon that most girls dream about. If it were not for gifts from family and friends, there would not have been any honeymoon at all.

We rented a small apartment with an avocado green molded plastic dining set we purchased from Robert's uncle for $50 dollars, a borrowed sofa, and a huge 25-inch television that showed a partial picture most of the time. Fortunately, we both had the exact bedroom furniture, so we combined his queen bed and nightstand with my dresser and had a complete set. We had all that anyone needed to set up house.

Love Is a Choice

A thriving marriage relationship is not based on a day, dress, cake, honeymoon, and what you do or do not possess. Success is not found in the traditions and celebrations surrounding your wedding, the bridal showers given in your honor, or the honeymoon you experience together. It is not based on the feelings enjoyed during the events leading up to your "big day" or your feelings on that day. It is not based on the first night together as you consummate your union.

Successful marriages are based on daily choices: to love and forgive. Success is found in giving even when it hurts and continuing to love despite your spouse's shortcomings. Love is a choice! Love is a daily choice! The butterflies may fly away, and, at times, you may not want to hold hands or even give yourself to each other! Life gets real and can be uncomfortable and difficult. However, your marriage will last because you choose to face the hard things together. You choose to love despite the challenges you face.

In a dream relationship, no one ever experiences hurt feelings or disagreements. However, the reality is that hurt feelings and disagreements happen. If you have been married for one day or fifty years, you probably know that these things are an unfortunate reality of married life. However, they can always be overcome with a simple choice to love with the *agape* kind of love that the apostle Paul speaks about:

> Love is patient, love is kind. It does not envy, it does not boast, it is not proud. It is not rude, it is not self-seeking, it is not easily angered, it keeps no record of wrongs. Love does not delight in evil but rejoices with the truth (1 Corinthians 13:4-6, ERV).

We must possess and practice these qualities and attributes for a lasting marriage. This is the only way love can grow, blossom, and be maintained. Love is not a feeling but an action we must practice every moment. Love is a choice we must make to experience a long, happy life with the person of our dreams. If we do not possess and practice the above characteristics of love, our dream will become a nightmare, which causes us to be afraid and run from the relationship. Some people will become defensive and attack their spouse like a home invader. Choosing to love the way the Bible prescribes is the best choice and will always bear good fruit.

Falling In Love vs. Choosing to Love

Marriages do not last and endure solely because two people "fall in love" with each other. They last because spouses choose to love one another. The emotions of love are not always present, particularly when there is conflict within the relationship. The only thing that has the power to enable marriages to succeed is the constant practice of love between each partner. I am referring to a ***sheer commitment*** love for one another regardless of the emotions that may be raging. We must learn to love through feelings of hurt, anger, sadness, and sometimes even rejection.

Loving your spouse is a deliberate action. Many people wait until they feel the emotion of love before they respond with any action of love. Those who do so will have a roller-coaster relationship; one day, they are on top of the mountain, and the next day, they are in the valley. Often, they will feel like the marriage train has derailed. Some people will suffer through the relationship, but more frequently, one partner decides to leave it. We must choose to love regardless of feelings. We must believe the best, give the best, and expect the best.

You should make a deliberate commitment to love your spouse every day, not because you feel love but because you choose to do so. The truth is that after we FALL in love, we must CHOOSE to love. A commitment to love your spouse is the one thing that will empower your marriage when everything else has fizzled out. Feelings come and go, but commitment to love is always the right thing to do.

Enduring the Challenges of Life

Every marriage will face challenges. Jesus said that in the world you would experience adversity and trials. The marriage relationship is no different since it consists of two people living in a fallen world. We all face difficult situations and circumstances. Every person will be plunged into moments that can make even the strongest individual want to throw in the towel and quit.

Your marriage will face adversity and obstacles at some point in time; every relationship encounters these things. I have heard my husband, Robert, say from the pulpit, "Welcome to Earth!" He and I have faced difficult situations repeatedly. The good news is that we are still together and going strong after more than forty years. If we can do it, you can too!

The first seven years of our marriage were the most trying times of our lives. Some seasons seemed easier to quit than continue. Marriage is work, but we had no idea just how much until we were already married. We both possessed strong personalities; many times, it was a war to see who would win. There were times when we were unsure if our marriage would succeed. Thank God that we finally learned a better way. God put people in our lives to help us better understand how to communicate and love one another in a way that was productive instead of destructive.

It is important to keep in mind that on the other side of the testing, there will be a testimony. Once the battle is over, there will be a story of victory. After the trial has ended, the devil will have another black eye. There is light at the end of the tunnel, and victory will be realized. Your love for one another will triumph and become stronger. Hallelujah!

Persistence is not a characteristic or quality of our human nature. This quality comes through the work of the Holy Spirit and God's Word being active within our lives. Our flesh may want to give up and throw in the towel. In the middle of conflict, the human desire is to run from conflict and pain. However, **we must learn to stop fighting in our marriage and start fighting for our marriage!**

The Language of Commitment

The greatest principle that will usher you into a breakthrough in your marriage is the ***sheer commitment*** kind of love. My husband expressed this precept when asked about the secret of our longevity in marriage. When you want to give up and quit, you must allow the grace of God to empower you to continue.

God desires to release this within us, but we must allow Him to do it and cooperate with Him. This may start with the removal of certain language from our vocabulary. We choose to remove words like "*I'm leaving*" or "*I want a divorce.*" This kind of language leads to separation and destroys marriages.

Instead, we must speak the language of love and commitment. We must look in the mirror and examine ourselves rather than point the finger at our spouse and blame them for a situation. We should join hands together while speaking words of affirmation to one another. The words coming out of our mouths should embody love, dedication, and commitment. Anything else should be a foreign language we cannot understand or speak.

Checking your own heart and motives before bringing complaints or accusations to your spouse is essential. Doing this will bring peace to your marriage and cause it to endure. Check yourself before you open your mouth to complain. Preferring your spouse is not always easy, but many times, it is not worth the struggle or fight to "have it your way."

So many times, we argue over things that are simply preference issues. Trust me, it is not worth the fight. Many times, I have been obstinate when I should have refused to make a big deal about a situation. Don't sweat the small stuff! Some things are just not worth the drama, hurt feelings, and division.

Love Like Jesus

Jesus didn't go to the cross because He felt like doing it. The reality is that He prayed that He would not be required to do so. However, Jesus' commitment to His bride, the church, was greater than the emotions and feelings of the moment. Jesus was committed to the wife that the Father had waiting for Him at the altar. The love Jesus exhibited was not based on emotions or feelings; it was based on obedience and commitment. Now, think about this: Husbands are commanded to have this same kind of love for their wives. Pause for a moment and let that sink in.

Jesus gave Himself for His bride, the church. The bridegroom was willing to do whatever was required to protect, heal, and bless her. This kingdom principle needs to be enacted within our marriages to keep them protected and whole. A successful marriage requires this type of commitment today.

Likewise, wives must give themselves wholly to their husbands holding nothing back. Since marriage is likened to the relationship of Jesus and the church, we, husbands and wives, need to do better at self-sacrifice. Jesus gave everything for His bride, and husbands are exhorted to model the same. Thus, wives are likened to the church and should submit, trust, and give themselves to their husbands while trusting that he will love and lead the way, as Christ does the church.

The Wise Marriage

Jesus shared a parable about a wise man and a foolish man. He said the wise man built his house (marriage and home) on a rock. When the storms of life came, his house stood. On the other hand, the foolish man built his house (marriage and home) on the sand. When the storms of life came, his house fell.

The Lord went on to say that the wise man was not only a hearer of the Word but also a doer of the Word. The foolish man heard the Word but failed to put it into practice. We must be like the wise man and build our marital relationship by hearing and doing what the Word says concerning marriage. If we do, when the storms of life arrive, our marriage will stand, and we will have a testimony of the grace and protection of the promise of the Word.

I have heard my husband say before that the wise man and foolish man went to the same church and even sat beside each other on the same pew. The only difference between the two was that one committed to do something while the other only gave the preacher an "amen" while listening. He failed to put anything into practice resulting in his house (marriage and home) falling to pieces.

Do What Is Right

The commitment to do what is right in your marriage relationship will cause it to stand when the storms of life come (and they will come). It is the determination that "come hell or high water," you will not surrender your home to the enemy of our soul. It is a constant and deliberate action to model the Word even if your spouse does not. This disposition will cause you to overcome the attack of hell and experience breakthroughs.

Attending marriage conferences and reading books (like this one) on marriage are good and helpful. They can strengthen and enhance your marriage and home while giving you a sound knowledge base and understanding of how to function. Ignorance is one of the leading ingredients to failure in any area of life. However, until you embrace the principle of ***sheer commitment,*** you will be vulnerable to the storms of life and spiritual attacks. You must become more than a hearer of the Word; you must become a doer of what Jesus taught.

Working to Make Marriages Succeed

It is critical to understand that no marriage will succeed without work. I recognize that work is a four-letter word, and many see it as a derogatory expression when discussing love and marriage. However, it is a biblical and godly word. In the beginning, God gave Adam a job and told him to work in the garden; he was given this commission before the fall of man. Work is something we were all created to do.

A man who does not work is never fulfilled. Recreation, play, and vacations are always fun and even needed elements in a relationship. However, we were all created to be productive and to work. God gave Adam and Eve a job to fulfill together; He told them to be fruitful, multiply, and subdue the earth. This means that some form of work and effort accompanies everything we achieve.

It is amazing how many people have no problem going to work every day to receive a salary. However, they fail to understand the necessity of working on their marriage to receive the payout of a successful relationship. In their minds, working for money is common sense, but working on a relationship should not be required for it to succeed. The attitude is that if their marriage was designed to succeed, there would be no need for working to see it bettered. However, nothing could be further from the truth.

Effort Is Needed

It takes effort and work for anything we do in life to succeed. Our relationships are no different. Marriage is not something we can put on autopilot, hoping that we arrive at our desired destination. Rather, it is something that we continue to work at and improve until we take our last breath.

Everything in life requires some measure of work for it to succeed. Nothing flourishes without labor. God promised that He would bless the work of our hands; He did not promise to bless the sitting on our bottoms. God will bless where people apply themselves and are diligent. He said in Proverbs that the hand of the diligent would be blessed and made rich (Proverbs 21:5). Many today do not have rich marriages and relationships with their spouse because they do not work at it.

Your marriage is worth the investment of work. The dividends will be great for those who commit wholly to their relationship to see it become mature and bettered. Those who do not work will ultimately see their marriage crash in the same way that the foolish man watched his house crash. Think about it!

Great Marriages Are Forged

Strong marriages do not automatically happen because you just happen to marry your perfect match. The truth is that great marriages are forged. I have yet to see any spousal relationship come into full fruition on their wedding day. On the contrary, the moment that you are pronounced husband and wife is the moment the work begins. You are merely at the starting line; you are just in the beginning stages. The race has just begun, and there is a course to be run. Sadly, many choose to run a separate track that divides them rather than choosing to run the course together, encouraging one another along the way.

I recognize in the modern hoopla surrounding wedding ceremonies, there is a tremendous amount of stress and work leading up to the big day. However, that pales compared to the time and investment necessary for a marriage relationship to succeed. These things are not said to make you dread marriage, but there does need to be a sober assessment of what is required for your marriage to succeed.

Great relationships are forged and formed; they do not happen solely because of a beautiful ceremony. The union is not perfect because you had the perfect wedding. The pastor's pronouncement of husband and wife is not a magic wand that seals things eternally. ***Sheer commitment*** is the only thing that will cause your marriage to stand the test of time. A commitment to be better individually, as well as together, to continue to love and forgive when life gets hard must be had.

No Lucky Rabbit's Foot

There is no lucky rabbit's foot that is going to cause any relationship to succeed. Many biblical principles need to be enacted to have the kind of marriage that God desires for your life. However, there is one principle that, if absent, will undoubtedly cause any marriage to fail. That is the principle of ***sheer commitment.***

I encourage you to embrace this principle today. Commit to your relationship. Work on your marriage by being the best spouse you can be. Refuse to live with the idea that you married the wrong person and, therefore, your marriage is doomed to fail. Renew your mind to what God said concerning your marriage, which includes "Let no man separate." Refuse to allow even the thought of separation to enter your mind; cast down every vain imagination.

You and your spouse are one. God made you to be together and enjoy one another. Maintain an attitude that you will work on your relationship by working on yourself. Refuse to point the finger but be willing to look in the mirror. Allow God to birth the principle of ***sheer commitment*** in your heart. You will surely see success and happiness as you both do these things.

Ask Yourself

Ponder on these things for a moment. Are you working to see your marriage succeed, or are you merely complaining about what is unpleasant? Are you willing to do what is right to see your marital relationship become fruitful, even when it is uncomfortable? Will you choose to love even when you do not feel like it? These things are key to seeing happiness in your relationship. Marriage is more than a day noted on a calendar; it is a lifetime commitment to work and develop together. It is truly a ***sheer commitment***!

4
Opposites Attract

My husband, Robert, and I grew up in similar homes. We were both raised in a Full Gospel Pentecostal church, and our families were average middle class. My dad worked hard to make a living for our family, as Robert's father did for their family.

Robert's fraternal grandmother, a godly woman, lived with them until he was seven years old and after that, she lived only a few houses down the street. Similarly, I had a godly grandmother who was involved in my life and whom I loved very much. Coincidentally, Robert's maternal grandmother and my fraternal grandmother went to the same Assembly of God church together and knew each other well. Our early lives were similar.

Robert and I were both raised in the same city on the east side of Bay County, Florida. We lived only one block away from each other until I was five years old; at that time, my dad built our new home. However, my grandparents lived only blocks from Robert and his family. We shopped at the same Piggly Wiggly® and probably passed each other many times in our cut-off shorts and dirty bare feet as little kids.

Robert and I attended the same junior high school and graduated from the same high school two years apart. Before we were married, we learned that we even had the same bedroom furniture. That's just how similar things were. Our parents even drove the same model of vehicle; one was a Pontiac, and the other was a Chevrolet. We both lived in block houses painted yellow. I cannot overstate how similar our backgrounds were. It is "freaky" to think about how close we lived to each other and the similarities we shared.

The Process Begins

Natural observation of these things reveals our comparable upbringing. However, we quickly discovered that while we shared so many commonalities, we thought very differently about almost everything. Once we were married, we seemed at times to be anything but similar, much less "one flesh." We were total opposites in numerous areas and did not become "one flesh" solely because we said, "I do" in front of our pastor, friends, and family.

Becoming one and being on the same page was going to be a process. It was going to take time, understanding, and conforming. We quickly learned that we thought differently and sometimes seemed to speak different languages. Unfortunately, neither of us were willing to admit or consider the possibility that we should regard the other. We were both headstrong individuals.

My father was easygoing and let my mom raise and discipline us. On the other hand, Robert's father was much the opposite and enforced most of the discipline in their home. Yet, in my home, my father was more passive. Neither is right or wrong, just different.

When we married, both of us had different views on how decisions should be made and carried out. Learning to compromise was not easy and took time to work out. Two individuals had to "become" one flesh. We had to create our unique way of doing things. It is not that our parents were wrong in conducting family matters, but we were a new family; we were now "us!"

> And the LORD God said, "It is not good that man should be alone; I will make him a helper comparable to him" (Genesis 2:18).

After God created Adam, He recognized that man was incomplete by himself. So, God made another individual to aid and complement the man He had made; that creation was called woman. She was God's final masterpiece that would enable Adam to fulfill everything he was commissioned to do. They would be a team that worked together to advance the purpose and plan of God. It would require them both to labor together to accomplish this. God made it clear that neither could do it alone. Likewise, you and your spouse need one another to achieve all God has planned for you.

Not a Clone—A Puzzle Piece

Eve was not created to be a clone of Adam; she was unique and different. The Hebrew word translated as "helper" is *neged*, which means to stand out boldly opposite. God made a creature who was the opposite of Adam.

For man to be complete, he needed an opposite. He did not need another individual who was exactly like him; he needed someone different. Robert and I were the perfect example of this. If you looked up the word *neged* in the dictionary, you would most likely find a picture of him and me. We were different in every way! To say that I stood out boldly opposite was the understatement of the year. I was the literal expression of that description constantly and not always in a good way. To describe us in about every area of life, one could say that sparks flew, opinions were opposed, and emotions ran high.

The Bible says that iron sharpens iron, and when this happens, sparks fly. That was us! Sparks were continually flying, and many fires started needlessly as a result. I felt as though we were in a constant sharpening process. God was shaving off the rough edges. Wrong attitudes and ideas were being adjusted so we could become who He called us to be and accomplish His plan together.

God designed man and woman—husband and wife—to fit together like a puzzle. The characteristic that makes puzzle pieces fit together is that they are inversely opposite. If they were identical, they would not fit. Being inversely opposite allows the pieces of a puzzle to form the beautiful picture it is designed to manifest. Likewise, when a husband and wife conclude that their differences are meant to complement one another, their lives together can become the manifestation of the glory of God.

Appreciate Your Differences and Embrace Them

How many times have we heard that opposites attract? It is true. Here is the wonderful thing: God made it that way! God designed for opposites to be attracted to each other when He made man and woman. God did not clone Adam and then call her Eve. He created her to fit as the opposite of man. Being different, we have unique roles and functions within the marriage relationship.

It is essential to appreciate and embrace our differences. A husband should recognize that his wife is different and embrace it. A wife should acknowledge that her husband is different and embrace it. A husband should not attempt to make his wife a man. Likewise, a wife should not attempt to make her husband a woman. We must embrace the distinctions we possess and celebrate them.

The truth is that as similar and compatible as you think you are before you get married, there are still many areas where you are the opposite. This truth can be attributed to a number of biological factors. However, the greatest one is that God made man and woman different in every way: physically, mentally, emotionally, and spiritually. While our uniqueness is what defines us as individuals, it can become a stumbling block in a marriage if we fail to recognize the need to adapt ourselves to one another.

When two people marry, the Bible says they become "one flesh." In many ways, that sounds so simple and wonderful, but in **real life**, it can be difficult. When two people from different families and sometimes what seem like two different worlds come together, there is most certainly the possibility of conflict and disagreements.

Becoming One Flesh

When God created Adam and Eve, He declared that a man would leave his father and mother, cleave to his wife, and they would become one flesh. Many have interpreted the phrase "one flesh" as something that takes place immediately when the pastor says, "I now pronounce you husband and wife." However, I have come to understand that becoming "one flesh" is a process. Becoming husband and wife occurred immediately around 7:30 pm on June 12, 1981, when Robert and I were married. Yet, there has been an ongoing process of becoming one flesh since that day over forty years ago.

It is much like becoming a Christian. The moment you make Jesus the Lord of your life, you become a new creation in Christ Jesus. However, the process of sanctification and being conformed to His image is an ongoing process within the life of all believers. It does not happen overnight; it is a life-long process for Christians to become Christ-like.

In the eyes of the Lord, the moment you say, "I do," at the altar, you are one flesh. However, the reality is a relationship begins with two opposites who are to become one. Two streams are designed to become one river. Two differing opinions must become united into one resolution. Unfortunately, this is not easy for us to do as human beings.

How often do we hold on to our opinions and preferences rather than allow adjustments for the sake of unity? How often do we fight to defend our position rather than yield to become what God said we were to be: one flesh? It can be challenging for those like me who possess strong opinions and preferences. However, this is what is required if we are going to live as one flesh. Otherwise, we become two ships passing in the night with no commonality other than sharing the same house, the same bed, and possibly the same checking account.

We Need Each Other

If you ever watch any sports teams, it's evident that there are players with different skillsets. In football, the quarterback can do things the wide receiver cannot. The wide receiver can do things the quarterback cannot. However, without a great wide receiver, a great quarterback will only be average at best. Without a great quarterback, a great receiver will never have the opportunity to excel. They need one another to maximize their potential.

In the football analogy, each player's different abilities and skillset give them the greatest potential to win the game. If the whole team could pass the ball, yet no one had the ability to block the defense, the quarterback would be sacked on every play. The offense would be inept. They would lose the game.

The marriage relationship works in the same manner. God creates two opposites to be together so that they can maximize each other's potential. The husband needs the wife, and the wife needs the husband. They cannot totally fulfill and maximize their abilities without one another.

The Bible says **one** puts a thousand to flight, but **two** puts ten thousand to flight. My husband always tells me that I'm his nine thousand! And likewise, he is my nine thousand! This biblical principle is spiritual synergism. The fact is that we need each other. To think that you can do it all by yourself is arrogant. You need the opposite that God made for you!

Difference Is Not Your Enemy

Many marriages are losing in the game of life because they fail to appreciate their differences. They see their spouse's unique characteristics and qualities as irritants rather than a blessing. They look at every differing opinion or preference that their spouse holds as an enemy combatant that challenges the control and hold of their territory rather than seeing it as something that completes their relationship. They fail to understand that their uniqueness is the quality that gives them the ability to win together.

It is so important for husbands and wives to abandon the idea of competing and embrace the principle of completing. Too many are living in a world of competition with one another. They wrestle with one another over differing ideas and see them as an assault. As a result, their marriage becomes a place of competition where two people battle on the field of play. The only opponent they possess is one another.

These things happen because of the failure to embrace the truth that God made us different so that we could complement and complete one another rather than challenge and compete. If couples can flip this perspective, it will make a remarkable difference in their relationship. They will have a marriage made in heaven rather than one made in… well, you know.

Winning Redefined

Winning in marriage must be redefined in our minds for our relationships to succeed. Winning cannot be defined as "*I won the argument*" or "*I got my way.*" If it is characterized in this manner, you will lose. Why is that? It is because, with those definitions, there will always be a loser: the other spouse. Hear this: if your spouse loses, you lose, too!

Once two people are married, they must understand that winning and losing is something they do together. The only way one can win is for both to win. They are on the same team. The opposing opinions and preferences in the relationship are meant to make them win together, not have a winner and loser, as one opinion triumphs over the other. You and your spouse are designed to be on the same team and prevail together.

If the perspective is that spouses are competing and on opposing teams, it will create a volatile atmosphere in the home and family. Spouses will be at each other's throats and view each other as enemies. Husbands will view their wives as the old ball and chain. Wives will view their husbands as self-centered jerks. This behavior is not the way God designed the marriage relationship to exist. He desires that we be one heart. He declared that the husband and wife are one flesh! (Genesis 2:24, Matthew 19:5-6, Mark 10:6-9).

Your Marriage Is Not a Sitcom

The fact is the only way that you win is if you win together. We must put away the television situation comedy (sitcom) ideas that have been around for decades, portraying husbands and wives at war with one another, even though they finally kiss and make up at the end of each episode. Unfortunately, there have been all sorts of negative ideas propagated in these television shows about the way spouses should treat one another.

In these sitcoms, fathers and mothers are often portrayed as ignorant and stupid, while the kids embody all wisdom and knowledge. This portrayal is not only unbiblical, but it chips away at the design God established for families to function properly. These shows do not model successful Christian marriages and homes.

Do not pattern your relationship after contemporary television dramas and sitcoms. These are merely Hollywood scripts performed by paid actors depicting dysfunction with attempts to get laughs and gain television ratings while normalizing poor marital behavior. We must use the Bible as the script for our marriage. When in doubt, refer to the playbook of marriage and family, the Word of God, or seek counsel from a godly pastor or counselor.

My Way or the Highway

An important principle that every marriage must embrace is that of flexibility. Each spouse must be flexible enough to bend regarding preferences and opinions, yet unchangeable relating to godly principles. The biblical principles that every marriage should be built upon are non-negotiable. However, methodologies and preferences are always subject to change and adaptation. We are married to our spouse, not our ideas and opinions.

For two people to become one, they must both abandon the idea of "my way or the highway." This attitude will destroy marriages or cause one partner to live in misery while tolerating the control and manipulation of the other. Staying together for the long term is not the only goal in marriage. Loving your moments together and creating lasting memories to pass on to generations to come is the goal. No joy can be found in a marriage where one is bound to the opinions and preferences of the other. That is not God's idea of becoming one flesh.

The apostle Paul specifically said that we are to prefer one another. That is a mark of spiritual maturity. Since selflessness is a principle of Christian growth, it is undoubtedly a key to maintaining a blossoming marital relationship. Being inflexible within your marriage will cause contentions and quarrels, which gives place to both the devil and the workings of the flesh.

Flexible things bend, but rigid things break. The truth is that failure to bend in your opinions and preferences is a primary ingredient to breaking up a marriage. The greater the flexibility, the more both spouses will conform to one another and become one flesh. The greater the rigidity, the more each spouse stands independently and fails to operate as a team. They may end up staying together, but they will live feeling broken and miserable.

Be Their Lover, Not Their Parent

Women should understand that their husbands did not marry them to have another mother. It is not the responsibility of a wife to mother her husband. If you want to turn your husband off quickly and get him upset, just treat him like he is your child. When a wife treats her husband in this manner, he will shut down. The process of becoming one flesh is aborted amid this type of behavior.

The same thing applies to husbands. A man is not to be his wife's father. In the same manner, she will abhor this kind of treatment. The reason for this is because it is out of order. Husbands and wives are not to rule over their spouses. God's design is that they become one flesh and rule together in their home and family. While each spouse has a different role, rulership and domination are not to be played by either one in a spousal relationship.

A wife must be her husband's lover, not his mother. A man must be his wife's dearest friend, not her father. Neither husband or wife are equipped to conduct these other roles in a marriage. They are to love one another, affirm one another, and work together.

You're Compatible Because You're Opposites

Years ago, a lady came into our office and said, "I don't believe my husband and I are compatible." As I dug deeper, it became apparent that she believed this because they always disagreed. They fussed and argued about everything. They had great difficulty getting on the same page, seemingly about anything and everything.

I finally told her that what she described was the very thing that made them compatible. Their problem was they did not understand how to turn those differences into positives to bring out their tremendous potential. We must throw out the idea that compatibility means we are identical. Actually, what makes you compatible is that you are opposites!

Is this not a frequent problem within marriages? We disagree with the furniture placement in our homes. We differ on what the daily routine should be with our children. One spouse had parents with little structure in the home, while the other spouse had parents who were regimented and seemed to be obsessive-compulsive. Each spouse enters a marriage with different ideas of how things should be conducted in the household. As strange as it sounds, that is what makes you compatible. Your differences act like magnetic poles that attract you to one another. One of you will be the North Pole and the other the South Pole.

Being Moldable Makes You Compatible

Having a wonderful marriage requires us to redefine what it means to be compatible. It does not mean that we have identical thoughts about everything. Becoming one flesh does not happen because you are exactly the same, but rather because you are willing to bend and be molded to fit into your marriage relationship. This is the process of becoming one flesh. Being identical does not make you fit together; being moldable is the quality that makes you compatible.

Instead of trying to make our spouse the person we want them to be, we must work on being the person they desire. If we spent more time looking in the mirror than pointing a finger at their perceived flaws, our relationships would thrive. The reality is that all of us have quirks. All of us have less-than-desirable attributes. There are no perfect people. However, we can choose to love our spouse regardless of any imperfection.

The process of becoming one flesh begins with two opposites being attracted to each other. As the relationship blossoms, it becomes the seedbed for love to grow and mature. Love is never realized to its fullest in moments and circumstances that are pleasant but rather in times of challenge and change. When your preferences and opinions are challenged, and you must bend to produce unity, love must work the most.

Fighting or Fitting

As I said earlier, Robert and I were raised similarly. We both loved God and desired to serve Him. However, once we were married, the real work of love began. It became apparent that with all our similarities, there were even more differences.

Once married, we had to make choices. We could either fight for our way or be willing to become one flesh. For a long time, we fought each other in our youthful ignorance. We finally realized that God's design and plan were totally different; we decided to stop fighting and start fitting. You are either fighting with one another or fitting with one another. Fitting is much better.

Allow God to work in your marriage. Embrace your differences and appreciate them. Let the iron be sharpened, but don't allow the fires to burn you. Recognize the value of your spouse, and remember that you are worth more together than alone. Becoming one flesh is a process and a journey worth taking. Stay the course, enjoy the ride, and savor the reward.

Ask Yourself

Consider and ponder for a moment: Are your spouse's differences appreciated or irritating? Do you see your partner as one called to complete you, or are you competing with them? Are you fighting to demand your way, or are you fitting to do things God's way? Are you willing to become one flesh within your marital relationship? These are things we must answer honestly and then make adjustments where needed. This is ***sheer commitment*** at work!

5
Who's the Boss?

How many times have you heard someone say their spouse is the boss in their relationship? Sometimes, people can say it in jest, but some are very serious. I know that my husband has even said, when asked a question that needed him to consult with me, "Let me talk to the boss lady." His intention was not to communicate that I was the boss but merely that he needed to talk to me before he made a commitment. However, there are constant power struggles in many marriages to see who can control it.

Within relationships, there is sometimes an ongoing fleshly manipulation for one spouse to gain the upper hand over the other. It becomes a matter of competing and jockeying for position. Things will be deliberately done for one to get their way. This is not the way God designed marriages to work. These sorts of things should not be ongoing within a family.

Maturity Needed

Let's talk about the beginning. I'm not talking about Adam & Eve; I'm talking about me and my husband, Robert. We married when we were young. I had just graduated from high school, and he had two years of college under his belt. We were ready to take on the world. At least, that is what we thought.

Although we were "in love," we had much growing and maturing to do. We knew two things: We both loved the Lord, and we loved each other. However, as I am sure you have heard, "Love is a verb." It is an action, not simply a feeling. Although love can possess feelings, they are not the totality of it. Emotions are only what is at the surface. The feelings of love will only take you so far in any relationship.

After over forty years of marriage, I can truthfully admit that we were "young and dumb" when we first married. We thought we knew it all, but we were far from knowing much about anything. Our relationship was weak, yet we felt indestructible. Much growth and maturing were needed, especially relationally. We had all the emotions of love and fondness but had not learned how to love when the feelings stopped.

Had the Lord not supernaturally sustained us, we would have failed. If Robert and I had not possessed an attitude of ***sheer commitment***, our marriage would have crashed. We just determined that we were not going to be another divorce statistic. So, we suffered through many things needlessly because of our ignorance, stubbornness, and pride. Yet, we did it because of determination and commitment. What a paradox!

Different Homes with Different Examples

Again, Robert came from a home where his dad was the head of their home. Rules were made and enforced by him. There was little room for any deviation.

On the other hand, I came from a home where my dad was laid back, and my mom was happy to go along with his adventures. I never remember seeing my father angry or upset. My mom shared her philosophy often by saying, "*Your dad works hard all week, so if he wants to do something, we do it.*"

Neither family was necessarily wrong in the way they handled things. There was nothing improper about either household. It was merely different homes, different lives, and different people from varying backgrounds and personalities. However, once we were married, these differences became challenges that required resolution for our marriage to succeed.

Opinionated, Persistent, and Headstrong

With all that said, I don't think I got the "happy to go along with whatever" trait from my mother. Some people have said that I'm opinionated, persistent, and headstrong, especially early in our relationship. My husband was one of those who told me of my strong personality on numerous occasions. Many things factored into me being that way. Probably the most profound thing was **fear**. It was the fear of not being heard, fear of being controlled, fear of never being able to have an opinion, fear of losing my identity, and oddly enough, fear of not being loved.

I remember telling my husband, "I will not be your mama!" I did not make that statement because I believed Robert wanted me to be his mother and domestic servant. Nor did I say it because I didn't love and respect his mother. I said that in the sense of "*I am an individual with an opinion, and I want to be heard and valued!*" Unfortunately, due to my fear, he heard me say it many times, and it caused needless problems.

You see, I let fear control me rather than trusting that he loved me enough to hear me. In allowing my fear to speak, I felt I could control the situation. Unfortunately, the only thing fear can do is receive and instigate the undesirable. I had to learn many things concerning our relationship and how to do things God's way rather than the way of the flesh.

Ignorance Produces Struggles

Growing up in church, we heard much about salvation, living holy, heaven, and hell, but not so much about family relationships and living peaceably and in love together. We did not learn about God being the "boss" or the head of our lives together as husband and wife. I'm sure it was mentioned occasionally, but there was never in-depth teaching on marriage. We were not taught how to relate as Christians in our homes. Therefore, we struggled.

There was always a power struggle in our marriage. It was not because we did not love each other but because our home lacked proper order and understanding. Our own ignorance of proper ways to communicate and relate to one another produced needless conflicts. Again, we loved the Lord and each other; we just lacked understanding of who should be the boss. Jesus was the Lord of our lives individually, but somewhere, we neglected to make Him the leader of our family and let Him govern every part of our relationship.

Once Jesus becomes the true head of your home, power struggles will end. I'm not saying you will never disagree or have differing opinions. But, when you remove fear and replace it with trust, life becomes much better. You turn every situation over to Him. Life is not about who is right or wrong; life is about fulfilling His purpose and plan for you together, both husband and wife.

When making major decisions regarding our future and family, we never get off track when submitting to God's plan instead of our desires. His plan is always better. He is always the best leader. The Bible says to submit your ways to Him, and He will guide your path (Proverbs 3:6).

I Love Arizona, but…

Earlier in our marriage, when our children were young, my husband was given the opportunity to become the worship pastor at a large church in Scottsdale, Arizona. It was, by far, his ministry dream job! The church had wonderful pastors, a tremendous salary, studio musicians, a great kid's program, and an amazing congregation who were so loving and welcoming. We loved this place.

Robert traveled back and forth from our home in Florida almost every weekend for several months, leading worship and building relationships. I went with him on a couple of occasions, and we took our kids once. We all loved it. Again, it was a vibrant church with wonderful people; it was an excellent opportunity for my husband. It is an understatement to say that we were excited about the new prospects.

With all that said, it was finally time to house hunt. It was so exhilarating! All the houses were large and beautiful. The landscape was different than what I was accustomed to, but it was a welcome change. Robert and I flew out for the weekend as usual, except this time, we were going to commit and find our home. It would be the house where we would continue to raise our children as we embarked on this new life adventure. I remember my husband's excitement at the possibilities; everything seemed perfect. The weekend was wonderful, with powerful services and great fellowship. Again, it was a great place.

The But Will Save Your Butt

Later that evening, when Robert and I were alone at dinner, I had to tell him something I felt all weekend. It was totally the opposite of everything we had been planning and discussing. I had to share with him that I could not get peace about moving! I had to tell him there was a huge hand on my chest saying, "This is **not** My plan for you!"

I somehow found the words to express my feelings in a calm and fearless way. In the best way I could, I shared with Robert that this move was not the will of God. After hearing this, he was shocked. Needless to say, we had some very serious conversations that night.

Robert had always said we would not make any major decisions unless we were both at peace and could move forward in total confidence, knowing it was the Lord's will for our lives. So, we agreed that we would not make the move. He felt terrible because he had already communicated with the leadership at the church about our plans to move. We were both disappointed and unsure of where to go from there. However, we knew that God was in control, and we trusted that His plan was better.

Within a year, that church suffered a great loss due to some unlawful dealings of a congregation member. They lost their building, along with much of the congregation. Had we not heeded the sensing of the Lord and allowed His caution to weigh greater than our desires, we would have been right in the middle of it all. However, because my husband trusted what I sensed from the Lord, we were spared from the devastation and hardship we could have experienced.

This situation had nothing to do with the pastor, his wife, or their staff. However, it affected this entire local body of believers. Thank God this church is stronger today than ever, and the pastors are still doing great things for the kingdom of God. Thankfully, God foresaw the situation ahead and shielded and protected us from it.

Perfect Environment but Bad Decisions

It's easy to say Jesus is the "boss" or in total control of your home and relationship until you fail to get what you want or until things don't go how you thought they should. You see, things have not changed much from the beginning. In the beginning, God made man in His image and likeness, and then He created woman from man. The Lord said that they were to have dominion over everything. There was just one rule: Do not eat from the tree of the knowledge of good and evil.

Well, we all know how that went! The serpent whispered in Eve's ear. Eve whispered in Adam's ear, and it is all history from there. Then, the blame game began. Eve blamed the serpent. Adam blamed Eve, and later, he blamed God. Neither Adam nor Eve accepted responsibility for their decisions and pointed the finger rather than looking in the mirror.

Man and woman were placed in the perfect environment. They walked and communed with God every evening. However, they still struggled and ultimately failed to keep Him at the very center of their decision-making. Perfect surroundings will not guarantee that your decisions will be right if you fail to keep Jesus at the center of your marriage.

Similarly, the struggle is real in a world where we are being bombarded by news broadcasts, social media, and "influencers" who we do not know from Adam's house cat. Then, we must contend with the daily pressures of life. If we allow our focus to become something or someone other than the Lord, we will fall off the deep end into a world of independent living and thinking. That is the total opposite of what we should be doing.

We should pursue God's will and plan by seeking His face through prayer. We should possess an understanding of His will and purpose for our lives. We need to be planted and active in a local church, and open to wise counsel from our pastors and church leaders. I have seen far too many good people get off track and too many marriages fail because they are being influenced by the wrong people, wrong motives, or wrong voices. We must always allow Jesus to be our greatest influencer. Endeavoring to fulfill His plan for our life, marriage, and family should be done at all costs.

Be a Doer of the Word

To have a Christ-centered marriage requires each spouse to place Jesus and His Word as the priority of their lives. They must put Him above everything else. The Word of God must become paramount for both the husband and wife. That means that they commit to being doers of the Word, not hearers only.

The only portion of the Word of God that will positively impact your marriage is what you put into practice and apply.

Regardless of how much you know, only what you do is going to really make a difference. Quoting Scripture is great, but practicing the Word is much better. Far too many people today quote the Bible when it is convenient but do not practice a daily lifestyle of obedience that represents the Word and how we should conduct our lives.

The Bible has a lot to say about marriage and the home. If we follow God's master design for our relationships, we will secure a happy and joyful home. Inversely, failure to follow God's blueprint will only lead to pain and heartache. It is just that simple. Following Jesus and His precepts are paramount to a lifestyle that leads to peace, prosperity, and promise in every area of your life and marriage.

Ask Yourself

Ask yourself this: Is Jesus at the center of my marriage? If not, what must be done to make Him my focus and boss? Is there a power struggle in my marital relationship, and what can be done to avoid it? Honestly answering these questions can place you on the right road to making Jesus the center of your marriage. Make Him the boss and cease the power struggle. ***Sheer commitment*** to His way is always the best way!

6

Unpack Your Suitcase

This chapter is personal for me because I spent the first several years of our married life suffering from serious thoughts and feelings of rejection. Unfortunately, this caused me to set myself up to be rejected. I battled with thoughts of unworthiness, along with the fear of not being loved or received. Innocent things done by my husband were often received by me as a personal attack. I lived in much emotional torment.

It was challenging to wrap my mind around the thought that my husband wanted to be with me forever. I constantly worried that I would do something that would drive him away. Any marital conflict would send me into a tailspin of insecurity and fear. It tormented and paralyzed me from fully being who God called me to be, along with the wife and mother I so desperately wanted to be.

As we go through life, we pick up emotional baggage, both good and bad. We add those things to what we will refer to in this chapter as our **suitcase** because we all carry one. This baggage can weigh us down and cause us to view ourselves and others based on what we have experienced or perceived. We look at everything and everyone through the prism of our past encounters. These experiences shape us into who we become and what we believe about ourselves and others.

All the good occurrences combined with their impressions can leave us with great memories and add traditions to our relationships. However, painful experiences can cause fear and insecurities, potentially tormenting us. These fear-based things cause havoc in our relationships and hinder or abort the call of God on our lives if not identified and addressed.

Welcome to Earth

When we are born, we come from a safe place of warmth and protection in our mother's womb into a world of bright lights and loud noises. We are plunged into a cold and sterile environment with nurses and doctors assessing our vitals by poking, rubbing, and in some cases, putting tubes down our throats or needles in our soft little bodies. All of these things are saying, "Welcome to Earth." Birthing is a wake-up call to the real world of hurt, yet it is our only way to experience life. Truthfully, life will not only bring joy and happiness but hurt, disappointment, and even rejection at times.

This chapter is not about the hurt and trauma we all experience but how we can overcome the pain and disappointment it brings. It is about removing from our suitcase the unneeded things that confine us to the constant hamster wheel and negative patterns of life. These things keep us from becoming who and what we were created to be.

If we continue to dress ourselves from that suitcase of hurt, trauma, disappointment, hatred, or betrayal (to name a few), we will never be able to put on the true identity for which we were created. We must remove all the garments of pain to be the beautiful creation we were intended to be because these things dramatically affect our marriages. We were not designed to wear clothing of rejection, hurt, and pain but rather the wardrobe of love, blessing, and acceptance.

We are constantly given the opportunity to pack our bags starting at birth. Throughout our lives, people knowingly and unknowingly do and say things that have the potential to offend or hurt us. These encounters have the capacity to shape not only how we perceive ourselves, but what we believe others see in us as well. When we do not remove them, these beliefs are brought into the marriage relationship, whether good or bad. These things can ultimately produce adverse effects on the relationship with our spouse.

You Can't Read

When I was in the first grade, one of my classmates made a negative comment concerning my reading capability. From that day forward, I believed my reading skills were deficient because of one person's opinion. This event made me terrified to read or even speak in front of others.

One first-grade classmate said something to cause this insecurity. I do not even remember the person who said it, but it had a profoundly negative impact on my life. One classmate, who was learning to read just like me, caused me to be afraid as I packed those words in my suitcase of life.

Moving to 7th grade, we had to memorize and recite the Preamble to the United States Constitution in front of the class. I memorized it, but when it came to speaking in front of the class, I was paralyzed. You may ask, "*Why did you have that issue?*" It was because I dressed myself from the suitcase I had packed in the first grade. It was a garment called "*I'm not a good reader.*" Therefore, in my mind, I could not speak in front of my peers either.

Things I believed about myself had to be unpacked to write this book. I had numerous personal prophecies about writing a book, but until I dealt with these inaccurate beliefs formed years ago, I remained paralyzed. All the prophetic words in the world will not happen if you do not address the ungodly negative beliefs you are carrying. I had been dressed in this belief of deficiency for years. Therefore, I was held captive in this area of my life and purpose. However, I made a decision to remove that piece of clothing from my suitcase, and now you are reading this book. Think about it!

My Painful Experience

Unfortunately, I have experienced what a suitcase of heartache can produce in your life and marriage. Growing up in my home, I always felt loved, safe, and secure. My parents were in love, and I knew it. Never once did I fear or even expect my parents to experience separation, and certainly not divorce.

We were a close family and had fun together. My family had game nights, and we ate at the table together every evening. We took family vacations, and my parents took vacations together. They went on date nights alone and with friends. My mother was a wonderful and dedicated stay-at-home wife and mom. She always took great care of my siblings and me. My dad worked hard and diligently to make a comfortable life for us. We had every need met and enjoyed life together as a family.

Then, one day, during my senior year of high school, the year I was planning my wedding, I learned of the unthinkable that rocked my world. My father, the man I looked up to and loved dearly, was having an affair. He was unfaithful to my mother and the vows they had once made. I remember crying for days; it devastated me. It not only crushed me, but my mother was hurt beyond measure. He then moved out of the house, and they soon divorced. My father's actions wounded my mother to the core. He was her world—her everything. She loved him with every fiber of her being.

I remember thinking, "How can this be? Not my daddy! He loves mama; he loves us!" But it was true, and it did happen. It was awful! It was painful! I could not understand how this could have happened to our family. Why would he do such a thing to my mother?

My Suitcase Was Being Packed

My father unknowingly added to the baggage that I would carry for years to come. I had not asked for these garments to be added to my suitcase, yet they were. Grief, abandonment, shame, hurt, disappointment, fear, rejection, and so much more were added without invitation. Since my suitcase was now filled with these things, I began dressing in them as if they belonged to me. I carried them from the home of the hurt young lady to the home that Robert and I were creating as husband and wife.

Bringing this suitcase full of hurt, rejection, and all the past offenses and trauma caused much turmoil in our marriage. It was not because I was a bad wife, nor Robert a bad husband, but because of the garments I chose to wear from the suitcase I carried. Instead of "Everything's Coming Up Roses," everything seemed like weeds and thorns. Instead of "Happily Ever After," it was "How Long Before He Leaves Me?" I viewed things from a place of rejection, rather than love and acceptance.

Every disagreement seemed to entertain thoughts of divorce. I had a difficult time believing Robert would not do the same thing to me that my father did to my mother. Therefore, I was always in fight or flight mode. I set myself up to be rejected.

The Cage of Hurt and Unforgiveness

The hurt I endured held me frozen in time. It caused me to act and react from a place of pain and insecurity. The root was the experiences I continued to hold and embrace. Was it real and valid? Yes, it was! However, unpacking and addressing these things was required to move forward for the "Happily Ever After" life of which I had dreamed.

I remember days of arguments with Robert that were simply based on my fears. I held an expectation that he would leave me in the same way my father left my mother. I felt unworthy of being loved, even though I had done nothing to cause that feeling. At the same time, I desperately wanted to be loved and to feel safe and secure.

I was wearing garments of hurt and rejection, yet I could not understand the dynamics. I wore garments of protection and self-preservation that were unneeded because my husband loved me and had no intention of leaving me. I projected my pain and insecurities onto him and did not even realize what I was doing. The hurt I experienced, along with associated unforgiveness, held me in a cage of fear and anxiety. I was imprisoned in a cell never intended for me.

Out of Control

There were days and nights that I felt out of control. So, I controlled my surroundings with actions manifested through anger, fear, and self-pity. I felt this constant war because of the garments in my suitcase. I recall wanting to die because I believed Robert deserved someone much better than me—someone who was not broken—someone other than me. Yet, I had dreams of our future together with the family and life we would share. I was living in constant turmoil because I was dressed in past hurt and disappointment that came out of my suitcase of life.

Our first several years of marriage were no walk in the park. Even though my parents were reconciled and remarried during the first year of our marriage, the baggage had already been packed. Just because they reconciled did not mean that the abandonment, fear, rejection, and other emotions just disappeared. Unfortunately, these garments had already become a part of my everyday wardrobe, and I continually chose to wear them. Ultimately, I had to intentionally recognize, sort, and unpack them from my life.

Reversing the Plan of Satan

It is the enemy's plan to use your past experiences to produce false beliefs and expectations about the people you love and, in turn, love you the most. It is his plan to cause mistrust, confusion, insecurities, and negative expectations in every relationship you encounter, especially your marriage. If these issues are not addressed, it will cause you to project these things upon your spouse, thus experiencing "hell on earth" rather than heavenly bliss.

When these dynamics exist, you become convinced they will do the same thing as those who previously hurt you. You will begin to view everything your spouse does through the glasses of your past experiences, even though they give you no cause. To move forward, we must unpack our garments of hurt and disappointment and replace them with a wardrobe of peace, joy, and fulfillment in our relationships.

Forgiveness is the Key

Jesus gave us a way to unpack all the hurt and trauma that life has dealt us; it is called forgiveness. John 20:23 says, "If you forgive anyone's sins, they are forgiven; but if you hold back, they are held back" (TLV). To "forgive" is the process of releasing someone from the responsibility of actions that hurt or offended us. This is necessary, not for the person who brought the offense but rather for the person who was offended or hurt.

Jesus said if you hold back (refrain from extending) forgiveness, then their sin is held. It does not say the offender holds it; instead, it is held by the offended. Meaning that the one suffering the offense is left holding the sin. Another way of saying this is that we are left holding the baggage.

In Matthew, Peter asked Jesus how many times he should forgive his brother (Matthew 18:21-35). Jesus told him seventy times seven and followed this up with a parable concerning a servant who owed a great debt that was forgiven by his lord. However, that same servant did not forgive his fellow servant for a small debt. When the lord found out about it, he reprimanded the servant for not forgiving the small debt when he had been forgiven a much larger one. The lord commanded that the unforgiving servant be turned over to the tormentors. Jesus said this is what happens to those who choose not to forgive; they are tormented.

Torment Caused by Unforgiveness

I was being tormented and did not even realize why. I was living daily with thoughts of rejection, abandonment, insecurity, and every negative emotion. My pain was not from what others did to me but from unconsciously holding on to unforgiveness. I was left holding the bag. I was being tormented, and thus tormenting others, by holding on to the bag of sin that had been committed against me, my mother, and my family through my father's actions. Since I had not forgiven him, I was being tormented. My past hurt produced present fear, which brought torment to our marriage.

Once I realized the enemy's plan and began the process of releasing and forgiving my father for the hurt he brought, I began to view things from a different perspective. I no longer lived a life of negative expectations, which I then projected on my husband. I started to see my future, and it was bright. I saw my "Happily Ever After" when I unpacked the suitcase that carried the baggage of hurt and pain.

The bag that once carried the sin of my father was now replaced with a future for which I had dreamed. It is a future now being lived out to its fullest, with my greatest dreams being fulfilled. Forgiveness will always free you from a life of torment. It all starts by choosing to release it and letting it go.

I Saw It Happen

I watched my mother go through this process when she remarried my father after their year-long divorce. Forgiveness was a choice she made and successfully navigated. As a result, trust and love were restored, and her health was revived. I watched her unpack the hurt placed in her suitcase as she loved my dad like he never did anything wrong!

My dad passed away in 2002, yet they were in love until the day he took his last breath. During difficult times, she loved and cared for him. She showed me what unconditional love looked like. My mother lived "for better or worse, in sickness and in health, 'til death do us part." She loved my father deeply, and he loved her!

Although my dad has been gone for many years, she still speaks of her love for him and how he was everything to her despite the difficulties through which they walked. Forgiveness was the key to their restoration. It is the key to deliverance and freedom from any past hurts.

Healing and Deliverance

In the early 1990s, Robert and I were introduced to a couple who were instrumental in bringing an understanding of how our belief systems are shaped about ourselves, each other, and even God. They assisted us as we walked through a process of forgiveness. We unpacked a myriad of things life had thrown at us from when we were little children until then. Their ministry was life-changing! We unpacked and offloaded all the ungodly things we believed because of varied life experiences. We replaced these ungodly beliefs with what God's Word said about us.

You see, the enemy has a counterfeit plan for your life. His desire is for you to believe the lies that you will always be who he says you are. However, God has a different plan found in His Word. Therefore, we must repack our hearts and minds with what the Bible says about us.

When I felt rejected, God said I was accepted. When I thought I had no purpose in life, God said He had a plan for me. When I believed I was deficient, He said His grace was sufficient for me. When I felt like a slow learner, He said I have the mind of Christ. When I felt fragile and vulnerable, He said He was my strength and refuge. When I said no one could love me, He loved me so much that He sent His Son to die for me!

For every lie the enemy throws your way, the Lord always has an answer to trump the devil's lies. We simply must believe what God says about us. We repack our suitcase by hiding His Word in our hearts so we do not sin. If we believe the lies of the enemy and act upon them, it is a sin. Therefore, we must continually fill our lives and hearts with His Word.

Breaking Life Patterns

When belief systems and life patterns are formed, you begin to think this is who you are and will always be. My eyes were opened, and I forgave my father for what took place in our family. I understood and resolved that none of this was done because of me, my mother, or anyone else. I realized that his failure did not mean it would automatically repeat itself in my marriage and family. As a result, I began to react and respond differently during conflict situations.

Our marriage is what it is today because we unpacked and ditched all the hurt and ungodly beliefs formed through traumas and negative life experiences of the past. We established new patterns of thinking, believing, and acting that brought about what we desired. It is questionable if our marriage would have lasted had we not ditched our old baggage.

Marriage is a beautiful institute designed by God. The Bible declares that a man who finds a wife finds a good thing and obtains favor from the Lord (Proverbs 18:22). The enemy wants nothing else but to destroy what God calls good. Scripture also says that one can put a thousand to flight, but two can put ten thousand. So, when a husband and wife are in agreement, nothing is impossible.

Choosing to Let Go

If we choose to hang onto past hurts and other negative emotions, we will be tormented. It is much better to forgive than to live tortured lives, thus causing pain and frustration to everyone we encounter. Forgiveness frees you to live the life you were created to live. It is a life liberated from other's opinions, actions, or words concerning you. God created you to live in fulfillment, and His intentions for you are good.

God has a good plan and a purpose for your life, and this does not include torment. However, if you do not forgive others and continue to hold on to hurts of the past, you choose a life other than the one God intended for you. Forgiveness is always the right choice. It is not always the easy choice, but it is the choice that will produce good fruit in your life and joy for those you encounter. Choose to let go of the past and embrace your future!

A New Pattern of Living

Has anyone ever said, "*You are acting just like* ______." If so, how did it make you feel? Most of the time, these things are not complimentary. We recognize that it's not a commendation but rather a way of pointing out a negative attribute picked up from someone else. I know from experience that if we do not walk in forgiveness, we will emulate things we dislike in others. In other words, if you were raised in a home where conflict resolution was screaming and yelling, then most likely, this is the pattern you will attempt to follow. If you are not accustomed to others having an opinion, then you may tend to view an opposing point of view as a challenge to your leadership abilities.

The enemy attempts to divide and conquer our marriages and homes in many ways. One way is to view our spouse through the lens of someone who wronged us and exhibited a bad example for us to follow. This is why it is vital for us to forgive and receive healing. Forgiving others for wrong behavior is a daily choice we must make to keep from emulating negative and ungodly conduct.

It is proven that if forgiveness is not enacted, the abused will become the abuser. Forgiveness is the knife in the hand of the surgeon that cuts away the hurt of the past. It liberates the one who forgives from continuing the same pattern of offense. Renewing our minds and receiving emotional healing will keep us from repeating sins committed against us. This is the way we break ungodly generational patterns that destroy marriages and families.

Time for a New Wardrobe

It is vital to unpack your suitcase. If not, you will always be dressing yourself in the emotional hurt, trauma, and disappointment of yesterday. It is the same as dressing in clothes that are out of style. You are a child of God, and those old clothes no longer fit you. You must forgive to rid yourself of that clothing. It is time for a new wardrobe of joy and peace. It is time for a relationship unhindered by the experiences of your past.

Wearing these new clothes results from daily decisions to live the life you were created to experience and fulfill the plan God intended for you to accomplish. Do not let the enemy's lies keep you dressed in the wrong garments. Put on the garments of praise as you forgive and move forward into fulfillment. God wants only the best for you, your marriage, your children, and your home. Live your best life by choosing to forgive. It is the right choice.

Ask Yourself

Ask yourself these questions: Are past hurts negatively affecting your marriage? Did things happen to cause pain and bitterness, which are now being projected onto your spouse? Are there people that you still need to forgive? If you answer "yes" to any of these questions, allow God to heal you. It starts by forgiving those who wronged you. It begins with unpacking your suitcase. This process is ***sheer commitment*** in action.

7

Jesus at the Center

From 1980 to 1987, Robert and I were privileged to sit under three pastors. They were all very knowledgeable about the Word of God, and each possessed a strong anointing to teach, preach, and minister the Word. They had prominent ministries and were anointed and gifted—both husbands and wives. However, all three of them ended up with fractured and broken marriages. It was sad to watch the enemy come in and destroy what seemed to be such powerful teams who were making a significant impact on the body of Christ.

You may ask, "*How can this happen?*" How can men and women be so gifted and anointed but end up with broken homes? While many factors can contribute to this dynamic, the most basic is one or both spouses failed to apply and practice God's Word concerning marriage. I know it sounds over-simplistic, but it is the truth. Anywhere there is divorce, there is a spouse (or spouses) not being a doer of the Word.

Being anointed by the Holy Spirit to preach, teach, sing, pray for the sick, and see miracles will not guarantee a successful marriage. Being able to prophesy and flow in the gifts of the Spirit is not the key to having unity within your family. Neither does being a Christian committed to a local church ensure that your marriage will thrive or even succeed. Obedience to the Word will produce greater things in your marriage than any anointing on your life.

He's Not the Center Without Obedience

Understand that being in ministry does not mean that Jesus is at the center of your marriage. Obedience to His commands concerning marriage and family is what places Him there. Preaching, prophesying, and praying for people do not denote that Jesus is at the helm of your home. Choosing to do what He commanded gives Him control. We must understand that Jesus cannot be at the center of our marriage if we fail to act like Him. Think about it!

Jesus only becomes the center of your home to the degree that you obey His Word. It is not because you prayed together and asked Him to rule and reign in your relationship. Jesus becomes the center of your marriage when His Word becomes the leading voice in your life. When that happens, power struggles between husband and wife cease; we live in peace and no longer strive for the navigator's seat in the marriage. We allow the Word to be our captain at the helm. We allow Him to take the wheel rather than just singing about it. This is how we make Jesus the center.

Commitment to Obey

For marriages to be successful, it is imperative that both husband and wife commit to following and obeying the principles and precepts outlined in God's Word concerning their relationship. This means that husbands will love their wives as Christ loved the church and gave Himself for it. It means that wives will love, submit, and respond appropriately to their husbands. This is the only way to have Jesus at the center of your marriage.

A husband should give everything to his wife in the same manner that Jesus gave everything to His bride, the church. A wife should give everything to her husband in the same manner that the church is to give everything to Jesus. We withhold nothing from one another. When I say nothing, I mean absolutely nothing is to be withheld. That is what constitutes a Christ-centered marriage. Only then is Jesus at the center.

The truth is that anything in life that neglects to place the Lord at the center will ultimately fail. He is our Rock and Cornerstone. At the end of the day, things not built on the foundation of being a doer of the Word will crash. Make Him the focus and foundation of your marriage.

Woman, Submit!

Many women have been fearful, just like I was, because of the Scriptures that designate the husband as the head of the house. The fear stems from misunderstanding Scripture, improper examples, and how it was taught and demonstrated. In the past, there have been those who have stood in pulpits and ignorantly used these Scriptures as a battle-ax against women and wives. Their intentions may have been good, but their fruit was bad.

Some Christian leaders exhibit knee-jerk reactions to some of the false women's movements that seek to pervert the roles of men and women. Unfortunately, an overreaction to error becomes error itself. Regardless of the reasoning, these things have resulted in toxicity among marriages. Husbands and wives did not know how to properly relate to one another because fear was at the helm, and Christ was not at the center. Jesus in the middle of your relationship means fear will have no place.

Not *I Dream of Jeannie*

When the Bible refers to a man being the head of his house, it does not mean that he is to be a dictator. It means he takes full responsibility for leading his family in the way of the Lord. He will lay down his life for his wife and love her with every fiber of his being. It does not mean he is to subjugate his wife to his every command.

A husband should treat his wife as he desires to be treated. It is the Golden Rule. This means that his wife is not to be his genie in a bottle like the old 1960s sitcom *I Dream of Jeannie*. She came out of the bottle to serve her master's every need and desire, then went back into it at his command. Not only is this kind of thinking archaic, but it is also unbiblical. It is demeaning to God's greatest masterpiece, women.

Eve was not given to Adam for him to possess a domestic servant. Neither was she given just for sexual satisfaction. Eve was given to Adam to be his companion and helper; she was there to assist him. God designed them to work together. Neither one was to lord over the other. They were created to complement, not control. A husband and wife should not have an up-down relationship where one dominates, and the other is subjugated. That is not the way that God created marriage to work!

Preferring One Another Is Key

The accurate understanding of Scripture both husband and wife should possess is preferring one another. We are commanded to do this. It is the greatest way to avoid power struggles within a marriage. If you prefer your spouse, you will not be fighting against them.

As a wife, I prefer my husband, which means I give greater weight to his preferences over mine. This is a biblical command to be followed by everyone (Romans 12:10, Ephesians 5:21). My husband, in turn, gives greater weight to my preferences than his. Why? It is because He loves me. We both choose to prefer each other.

Can you see how this causes the all-too-common power struggle to be dismissed from the marriage? We no longer demand our way. We do not shout at each other with the threat, "*My way or the highway!*" We willingly submit to God's way and prefer one another. This one principle will shift your marriage into a greater place.

It is essential for husbands and wives to develop a team mentality. This means that they work together for the betterment of each other and their entire family. They must learn to unite their perspectives rather than being adversarial. When Christ is at the center of the relationship, differing thoughts and ideas are meant to complete the picture, not divide one another.

Go to Church

Making Jesus the focus of your marriage means that church attendance and gathering with those of like precious faith is a priority. Family time is not defined as getting away from everything by camping every weekend. There is no greater family time than being in the house of the Lord and worshipping Him together. We not only go to church, but we also function and participate in the ministry and activities of a local body of believers.

There is an old saying I learned as a young girl which says, "The family that prays together stays together." It may sound somewhat contrived, but it is the truth. Participating in spiritual things with your spouse will strengthen your marriage and family. It will minister to every member and give focus to Jesus at the center of all you do.

Statistics state that **regular** church attenders are less likely to separate or divorce *(ifstudies.org)*. That is just a fact! Regular church attendance is a deterrent to the spirit of separation and divorce. It acts as part of your shield of faith that quenches every fiery dart of the devil.

There is strength and protection when other believers surround you. There is accountability for both husband and wife when they are connected to spiritual leadership within a local church. God designed it that way. If we do things His way, we will experience His blessing in our marriages and homes.

> Do not be unequally yoked together with unbelievers. For what fellowship has righteousness with lawlessness? And what

> communion has light with darkness? (2 Corinthians 6:14).

The way most believers interpret this Scripture is that everything will be fine if they marry another Christian. However, one of the four biggest causes of separation in marriages is conflict over religion. I have witnessed Christian couples with numerous problems in their marriage because they were unequally yoked. If one spouse passionately pursues the things of God while the other is indifferent, there will be issues in the marriage.

Husbands and wives need to be on corresponding and matching pages regarding the things of God. Differing perspectives on non-essential items may exist; there is always room for some variation. However, there should be agreement on the fundamental principles of Christianity and biblical values. This compatibility is crucial for couples to succeed.

In the previous verse of Scripture, Paul specifically stated that a believer should not marry an unbeliever. No Christian should ever knowingly marry someone who is not saved—period! The dynamic of believers and unbelievers forming an intimate relationship will assuredly cause problems. However, when two believers are not on the same page spiritually, this can equally cause negative issues.

My Story—Not Called, but I Love You

I recall a serious conversation Robert and I had before we married. This conversation was essential to our future marriage and destiny together. I remember sitting in his car as he began to share his heart and what he knew God had called him to do.

Understand, at that point, he did not realize the totality of all that would come, but he knew he needed to share it with me if we were going to consider marriage. I listened intently.

He shared that he knew God had called him to full-time ministry. Again, we had no idea what all this meant, but I had to be willing to fully buy into it regardless of what it meant or where it took us. I had to be willing to support the things he felt God was calling him to do. We had to be on the same page.

After he finished sharing his heart, he said that this was non-negotiable, and I needed to understand and support him in this if we were to continue dating and planning for the future. My response to him was one of total support, and I shared with him that I did not feel the same call to ministry that he did.

I had watched him and knew this was something about which he was passionate. The weightiness of this call on his life was apparent. I expressed my willingness to support him in what he felt called to do, whatever it looked like and wherever it led us.

At that moment, I did not feel qualified; thus, I could not feel called. Every pastor, youth pastor, or music pastor I knew had a wife who played the piano, sang, or could lead the choir. I could do none of it. I was just a young girl in love with a good-looking guy with all the skills, confidence, and ability. All I knew was that I could follow him to the moon and back and be happy by his side, supporting him in whatever and wherever God called him.

This conversation was vital. It was important for Robert to share his heart with me, and I needed to share my heart with him. I am thankful that we both knew where we stood and went into our marriage with eyes wide open concerning our future and where God was leading us.

Spiritual Unity Produces Good Fruit

For a marriage to experience the full blessing of God, both parties must be on the same spiritual page. Family devotions are great, but it is more important that there be spiritual unity. There needs to be agreement on being planted in a local church. There must be no division concerning spiritual matters within the household. Spiritual unity in a marriage will produce good fruit, the primary one being longevity in the relationship.

A lack of agreement will cause strife and division in marital relationships, even in households where two Christians reside. Some things may be negotiable, but some issues cannot be flexible. The facts that you must be born-again and that Jesus is the only way are non-negotiable. The truth that marriage is between one man and one woman is not up for discussion. Understanding the importance of being planted in a strong local church is not debatable. These things are truths that must be equally embraced by both spouses for there to be agreement. Failure to agree on these things can cause a breakdown in the relationship and eventually failure in the marriage. Spiritual agreement is of paramount importance.

Love Is Not Enough

Far too many young people think the feeling of love is enough and you will figure out the rest as you go. Nevertheless, I believe it is important to have clear expectations, goals, and at least a destination laid out. Even if the road to getting there is unclear, you should have some idea of where you are going. By doing so, you are, at minimum, on the same page together. It is much easier to enjoy the scenery when both parties are informed of the intended destination.

You must be open, honest, and crystal-clear for unity to thrive. It is impossible to be unified when agendas and motives are concealed from one another. It is essential to create the opportunity for each person to speak without prejudgment and walls; always strive to have open communication. We must also be receptive to being wrong. It is imperative to have open hearts and ears to hear our partner's feelings, concerns, and expectations. If our hearts are closed and we maintain a mindset of infallibility, we will never have a marriage made in heaven as we all desire.

It's Not About the Ring or the Thing

Robert and I shared in our local church during a month-long series on marriage about being equally yoked and the importance of church attendance and faithfulness. I shared a story concerning different people we had seen through the years who came to church simply because of the person they were pursuing. Their church attendance was not because of a relationship with the Lord; they were chasing the physical and emotional desires they had for a person.

As we ministered, a song came to mind, and I began to sing: "If you like it, then you shoulda put a ring on it." The congregation laughed. Then I boldly stated, "It should NOT be 'if you like it, you better put a ring on it,' rather 'If you love Jesus, then I'll let you put a ring on it!'" I continued to declare that they all like "IT," but do they love the Lord? There is an enormous difference. They think they are in love, and they may, but love will only last when you put Jesus first.

We need to get our priorities straight. If we are simply pursuing a physical attraction that fades and feelings that change daily, then our motives are wrong. I have heard it said many times that if you are in pursuit of a spouse, simply run after Jesus and His plan for your life. Then, look beside you and see who is running there. This is how you will find the one to whom you can be equally yoked.

It's HIM, Not him

Some ladies get caught up in the "him" and forget "HIM." For you women, it should be about HIM (the Lord), not him (a man)! If your relationship is based simply on physical attraction or what a person can offer you, then you will be, of all people, most miserable. The "him" and the "it" may have an excitement and thrill; however, one of the most important decisions made in life should not be based on things that fade, or else they will soon become common and despised. Contrastingly, a marriage based on the pursuit of Jesus and His plan for your lives together will last and remain fresh.

To be strong, Jesus must be at the center of a marriage; He is the author and originator of love. When our relationships center around Him, love will be the byproduct. Allow Jesus to be in control of your home and family. Exalt His will and purpose within your life. Choose to obey His Word even if it is uncomfortable. The fruit will be a lasting relationship filled with His presence and peace.

Ask Yourself

Ask yourself these questions: Will you commit to obeying God's Word within your marriage? Will you make His plan your pursuit? Will you place Jesus in the highest place within your marital relationship? Will you commit to preferring your spouse over yourself? If your answer is "yes," then you will see peace and unity. ***Sheer commitment*** to God's plan is the sure way to have a marriage that will last a lifetime.

8

This Is Not a One-Way Street

Marriage cannot succeed as a one-way street. It should not be two lives with separate agendas going two separate paths with two separate goals. A successful marriage requires both parties to work together. It is not a "give and take" proposition; instead, it is a "give and give" position. It is impossible to have a healthy, thriving marriage when either party constantly takes and never gives anything back. No single individual should solely benefit from a marriage; both should be givers and benefit from one another.

Jesus gave everything He had for His bride. He willingly laid down His life so we could experience something greater than we deserve. Marriage should be that way. Live to give to your spouse. You should pour your life out for your spouse so they feel loved, appreciated, and secure. That is the example Jesus set for us all.

When a spouse is consumed with their own desires and elevates them to a place of priority, relationships become a one-way street. If this happens, the other partner will feel taken advantage of and, in many cases, misused or even abused. This is the makings of disaster and devastation in a marriage.

Self-interest must be abandoned once two people say, "I do." If selfish desires are not put away, any marriage will explode. Unless we lay aside pride and narcissistic thinking, our marriages will become a one-way street where, eventually, someone drives in the wrong direction, resulting in a crash. Many marriages fail because of wrong thinking and selfish behavior. This is not God's design for the home. Your marriage was not designed to be a one-way street but rather a bidirectional highway. It is intended that both parties benefit as they allow space and grace for each other.

Willing to Sacrifice and Give

When we first married, we didn't have money to spare, but like most girls, I liked shopping—even if just to window shop. Well, my husband, who had no sisters, did not understand the concept of shopping without the intent or need to purchase something. This difference in thinking caused problems and attitudes early in our marriage.

I recall when we went to our local shopping mall, his face and attitude revealed his displeasure after about thirty minutes. I could not understand why he was not enjoying what we were doing and the time we were spending together, and he could not understand why I wanted to shop. It seemed to always end up in an argument and then leaving angry with one another. I was not happy, and he was not either. Thank God we finally realized the importance of giving to one another, even when it was sacrificial.

He tells it this way: "I hated shopping and had to learn to shop in order to have a happy wife." You know what they say, "Happy wife; happy life." There is truth to this statement. He had to lay down his desires to see mine fulfilled. This is what Jesus demonstrated. However, I also had to adjust and realize that there were limits to his sacrifice while pursuing my desires. We had to find a happy middle; we had to prefer one another. Now, he loves to shop, still within limits, but sometimes more than I do.

This example may seem carnal and trivial, but it's "the little foxes that spoil the vine" (Solomon 2:15, KJV). It is the small things that we can do differently that will make the biggest difference. It is the little attitudes that creep in and drive us apart. It is so important to be willing to give yourself, even when it is not what you like to do. Sacrificial living is part of marriage. Jesus not only demonstrated it, but He also commanded it.

It Takes Two

Understand this: It takes two working together for a marital relationship to succeed. A marriage requires two people who are willing to submit everything to the understanding and application of God's Word. We cannot arbitrarily pick and choose what we believe and practice according to what may benefit our argument or need at the given moment. Neither should the Bible be used as a weapon against our spouse or as a tool to manipulate situations to get our way. Both husband and wife must apply biblical commands to their lives for their marriage to blossom.

> Wives, submit to your own husbands, as to the Lord. For the husband is head of the wife, as also Christ is head of the church; and He is the Savior of the body. Therefore, just as the church is subject to Christ, so let the wives be

> to their own husbands in everything. Husbands, love your wives, just as Christ also loved the church and gave Himself for her (Ephesians 5:22-25).

If you are like me, this passage of Scripture has always been hard to digest. Why is this difficult when it is so simple and places responsibility on both parties of the marriage union exampled by Jesus Himself? If we look at the heart of what is stated, we will see mirrored commands of LOVE in ACTION! Jesus never requires anything of others that He does not demonstrate. Likewise, we should never expect anything from our spouse that we are unwilling to give. So many times, we want love and affection, but we only give cold shoulders and shade. We want understanding when we offer none. This action will never promote a place of peace in our marriage relationships.

The Law of Sowing and Reaping

The Bible tells us that whatever we sow, we will surely reap (Galatians 6:7). We love that promise when it comes to financial blessing, but not so much when it comes to our attitude and giving ourselves to our spouse. Often, we do not apply this biblical principle in how we treat and respond to our spouses. This verse should be our first thought when it comes to sowing. You may not always have financial things to sow, but you can always sow words of kindness and love. You can always give of yourself.

Imagine a marriage full of similar sacrifices. This is the kind of love in action that Jesus demonstrated and should be reflected in every marriage. What if we saw our marriage through the sacrifice Jesus made for us when He went to the cross and gave it all? What if we gave our all while holding back nothing?

We can see in the Scripture that there are equal commands for both husbands and wives. As stated previously, successful marriages are not a one-way street. Each party has a similar, yet different, responsibility in fulfilling the marriage covenant. Each person is commanded to love. However, that command to love is demonstrated differently for both.

Husbands Are Commanded to *Agape*

Let's first look at the kind of love the husband is commanded to demonstrate for his bride. The Scripture shows how a husband is commanded to love his wife as Christ loves the church and gave Himself for it. In other words, the husband is directed to lay down his life for his wife. This kind of love is the ***agape*** kind of love we find in 1 Corinthians 13, often referred to as the "Love Chapter." This unconditional love is the same kind Jesus demonstrates to His bride, the church. He gave her EVERYTHING!

The husband is commanded to give himself fully to his wife. Every man should make an unselfish sacrifice by prioritizing his spouse's needs. We see so many marriages today where boats, fishing trips, favorite sports teams, cars, trucks, dogs, and even the kids are the priority—making these things the priority will cause resentment and, ultimately, division in your marriage.

I am not saying that a spouse's hobbies or interests must cease to exist; they should just no longer be the priority. As a husband, like Jesus, your bride must be your first and most important priority.

For many men, this is a foreign idea. They never saw it demonstrated growing up. They never heard it preached in the pulpit. It was never the revelation that jumped off the pages of the Bible when they were in their study time. Therefore, grace must be extended as we learn.

We Must Follow the Bible

You may ask, "*How can I have a successful marriage? I've read every marriage book I can get my hands on!*" That is all well and good, but the best and only way to have a successful and fulfilled marriage is to follow the Bible. It should be our handbook for salvation, healing, and peace, as well as our #1 go-to book for a successful marriage, family, and life.

We must stop treating the Bible like Google® and using it as a quick fix for things we cannot quickly mend ourselves. We must let God's Word be the textbook for our daily life and marriage. We must use it as a life source—a doctor's prescription for an ailment. It is our source of peace, joy, and conflict resolution. It is our guide for love, proper relationships, and communication. It is even a handbook for our sex life and can help us understand our spouses' needs and desires.

When faced with opposition or problems, our first question should be, "*What does God's Word say about it?*" The Bible should be our marriage manual. If we allow it to be our final authority, our marital relationships will be successful and thriving. If we work the Word, it will not fail. Man can fail, but God's Word **never** fails. We only fail when we neglect to work His Word.

Many marriages do not thrive and often end in divorce, solely because they do not follow the Bible. Their relationships falter not because of a lack of attraction or feelings of love but rather the failure to work the Word when it comes to their marriage.

The Bible must be the standard for establishing our marriages and families. Many marriages struggle and end needlessly when one or both parties fail to obey the Bible's simple basic principles laid out for us to practice. It is a daily choice, and the enemy wants nothing more than to get us out of God's desired will and plan for our lives by getting us to neglect following God's marriage manual.

Bad Choices and Bad Voices

Many believers today suffer much turmoil in their marriages simply because of the choices they make. Some would rather get advice from friends who are single, or possibly from someone going through marriage issues, or the one who has been divorced and remarried multiple times.

Many will seek advice from those who are not Christians and have never even considered what the Bible has to say about marriage. Some may go to a believer but choose those not plugged into a local church or who fail to live as a believer should live. Others seek help from talk shows with excellent ratings and interesting guests, but if you knew the stories behind their lives, you would probably not want their advice. Their marriages are often filled with turmoil, and they are in no position to counsel anyone.

Just because someone looks and sounds like they have all the answers does not make them right. Jesus clearly said, "You will know them by their fruit" (Matthew 7:16). What kind of fruit do you see in a person's life? What does their family look like? Do you want what they are offering, and do they really have anything worth offering? The Bible also says to follow those "who through faith and patience inherit the promises" (Hebrews 6:12). Don't allow wrong and ungodly voices to influence your decisions.

A Pretty Face Does Not Fix Problems

It must be understood that social media and internet influencers have absolutely no track record or relationship with you or your situation. They are just a pretty face on a person's computer or phone screen that seems to have all the right things to say, or at least you think they do. They tell you how to act, react, and handle your marriage and family while their lives and marriages are in shambles. A pretty face does not fix problems. Simple words do not resolve issues. Putting your trust in man will lead you down the wrong path.

Have you ever considered that perhaps the ones you choose to listen to are in a similar or possibly worse situation than you? Have you thought that they are in denial and hiding behind their on-screen persona? Have you considered that they may not have it all together? Anyone listening to the wrong voices will make the wrong choices.

The Word of God and its application in your life is the only thing that will truly bring life to a dead and hopeless situation. It is the only thing that has the power to change what may seem impossible into something different, something good, and stories where dreams come true. Only Jesus has the power to save that which seems lost and hopeless.

We Have the Tools Needed

As Christians, we have every tool available to have successful relationships. Unfortunately, we often neglect to make it our first source of help in time of need. We want a quick fix that requires the least work on our part, relieving us of any responsibility and placing it on someone or something else. It is always easier to point the finger at our spouse, children, job, church, or some other random place, anywhere we can take the blame and responsibility off ourselves.

Is the reason we seek out these other voices because we have an issue that we personally need to address in our own lives? Perhaps it is one we need to adjust or even change. Think about it! Most people desire an easy fix; they want to hear, "*You are ok; your spouse is the problem.*" However, most of the time, it is not the truth. We must take an honest look at ourselves.

Following the biblical pattern is the only way to have a healthy, happy, and sustainable marriage. If we **obey** God's Word, then and only then will we have heaven on earth in our marriage. When we look to the world for answers, we will reap worldly results. The last time I checked, the world's track record for great marriages was not so great. However, if we follow the plan stated in the first and best marriage book, the Bible, we will have success.

Marriage is not a one-way street. Both individuals must work for the betterment of each other. They must be willing to lay down their own desires and preferences while seeking to fulfill their spouse. When both parties do this, marital bliss will be the outcome.

Ask Yourself

Ponder and think about this: Do you live as a giver or a taker? Do you expect things from your spouse that you are unwilling to do yourself? Will you let God's Word be the manual for your marriage? These things need to be considered for your relationship to have good fruit. It is through ***sheer commitment*** to live as givers, the way God has commanded us to live, that you will experience fulfillment and blessing!

9

Why Can't We Be Friends?

> The older women likewise, that they be reverent in behavior, not slanderers, not given to much wine, teachers of good things—that they admonish the young women to love their husbands, to love their children, to be discreet, chaste, homemakers, good, obedient to their own husbands, that the word of God may not be blasphemed (Titus 2:3-5).

Now, let's talk about the command for wives to love their husbands. There is so much to unpack in this very short segment relating to women in this BIG book called the Bible. On the surface, it seems somewhat out-of-date and old-school, possibly chauvinistic in today's world. However, when interpreted correctly, the Word of God is never outdated or irrelevant. The problem lies in the heart of each individual reading and applying the Word. When we fail to read and apply the Word properly, we open the door for the enemy to twist it and thus cause us to reject it.

Be a Friend

I want to address some things in this passage of Scripture that pertain to women today. So, let's first look at the phrase "**love** their husbands." The Greek word translated as love here is *philandros*, with the ***Strong's*** definition being a loving friend or the special affection of a woman for her lifetime mate (husband), embracing him as her calling (stewardship) from God. The root word of *philandro*s means friendly or loving. *Philandros* is where we derive our word philanthropy, which we understand to mean generous giving.

When we think of philanthropy, we think of people who use their resources to assist those in need. I am not promoting that your husband is a charity case and that he needs you to bail him out or fix him. However, he does need you to be his friend.

Imagine for a moment that we take our marriage as seriously as we take our "calling" from God. I see so many women today seeking ministry opportunities and platforms from which to preach rather than just loving their husbands and being a friend to them. As wives, we must realize that our husbands are our first and most important calling and ministry. What if you sought to minister to your husband the same way you desired to minister to the Lord and His people? What if you were just "friendly" to your husband like you are to the lost person you are attempting to point to Jesus?

Many times, we forget that Jesus loves our husbands. They are important to Him and should be important to us. What if you are the only Jesus he sees and knows? What if you truly love him the way Jesus does? The Bible clearly says this is our calling. Before the pulpits and ladies' Bible studies, are you ministering to your husband and being friendly to him? I am not saying these spiritual things are wrong, but we must ensure our priorities are right. If our priorities are out of order, our marriages will suffer.

Great Relationships Start as Friendships

I hear and see so many ladies needing their girl's night out rather than dating and being friendly with their husbands. The relationship with your spouse probably did not start as a romantic, passionate, or physical connection. It probably started as a friendship. Most relationships start because of shared interests or some personality trait and attraction. You were most likely friends before you were husband and wife, and then lovers. These are the things that were at the foundation of your relationship.

It seems that many spouses have forgotten how to be friends. They do life together, yet everything they experience seems transactional rather than friendship. They wake up, go to work, come home, eat dinner, and go to bed. Life becomes a grind, and they forget how to be friends. At the end of the day, if spouses cannot be friends, they are in for a lifetime of sorrow.

Ladies, we must remember that after our name changes and we become their wife, our first and foremost command is to be their friend. We can be the best homemaker, the best Sunday school teacher, the best mother, the best cook, the best housekeeper, and the best employee at our job, but if we cannot be our husband's friend, we are falling short of the foremost responsibility given to us as a wife.

Please don't misunderstand me. We should excel and do well in every endeavor we undertake. However, if our marriage suffers while all else succeeds, are we really successful? Getting things right in our marriage is of the utmost importance. We can accumulate friends and followers on every social media platform available, but if we fail to be friends with our spouse, we have missed the very essence of what friendship should be.

The Law of Kindness

The type of friendship or love that a wife is to exhibit for her husband is responsive. As women, we are commanded to respond appropriately to our husbands. Again, this means we should be kind and warmhearted. The Bible speaks of this type of wife, "She opens her mouth with wisdom, and on her tongue is the law of kindness" (Proverbs 31:26).

There is an old adage which says, "You can attract more flies with honey than with vinegar." This saying simply means it is better to be sweet than bitter. You can win over more people with words of kindness than rebuking or fault-finding. It is better to be sweet than sour. Your conversation with your husband should be like honey dripping from a honeycomb rather than a glass full of vinegar.

Your husband does not need you to be his mother, teacher, or corrector. He needs you to be his friend. He needs your affirmation, not your constant correction. He was not attracted to you because you were constantly nagging him. This kind of behavior will not endear him to you. He desires and needs you to be a friend. This is the way God designed the relationship.

You Need Not Feel Alone

Many women feel isolated simply because they neglect to be friendly to their spouses. They find fault and disdain for the very person they deeply loved at the beginning of the relationship. They push their spouse out of their lives, resulting in needless self-induced loneliness. Their own perspective of their husband produces distance in the relationship. These things should not be happening within Christian marriages and homes.

It amazes me how many couples spend so little time together. The wife seems to always be off with the girls or needing "me time." The husband is either heavily involved in sports or off with his buddies on adventures. I am not saying that you cannot have friends or spend time with others, but if it takes priority over time with your spouse, then you will have issues. This can become a dangerous trap of the enemy and drive a wedge between you and the one who is supposed to be your closest friend.

No one should ever be closer to you than your spouse. There should never be anyone, male or female, who is closer or more intimate with you. If anyone gets closer to you, then you have entered the danger zone. This is how inordinate and sinful relationships begin—through close friendships with those who are not your spouse. You must guard yourself and ensure that no one ever becomes a greater friend to you than the person you married.

Most women want to feel loved, appreciated, and valued. Men are no different. They may seem all rough and tough or big and bad, but deep down, they desire their wife to love them, spend time with them, and value them for more than just what they can do. They want a true friend and confidant with whom they share their deepest thoughts and emotions. They desire a person they can trust and share their aspirations and dreams. It should be you! Be your husband's friend.

God's Plan of Order

The apostle Paul declares that the husband is the head of the wife, just like Christ is the head of the church. God set an order in the home. He established that the husband is to be the leader and head. You have probably heard it said that anything with two heads is a freak. That is a true statement, and marriage is no exception. Unfortunately, we see this in many marital relationships. Not only did Jesus model something different, but He commanded something different.

Many marriages suffer because the head of the home is not properly established or not accepted and received. You may even battle with this in your own home. You may know the concept and command yet struggle at times with implementing this truth. This situation is not uncommon and can be resolved and corrected.

From my personal experience, I have discovered that this problem with headship is primarily due to fear. It is the fear of being controlled, the fear of being inferior, or the fear that your opinion and feelings will not carry weight. All of these things may be real, but we must be free, or it will prevent proper order in our homes from being established.

Overcome the Fear

As I shared previously, at the beginning of our marriage, I despised the word "submit." I hated the mental picture that was conjured in my mind when I heard it said. All I could see was a woman chained to a stove, washing machine, and kids. I perceived it as a word that meant I would be the target of domination. Truthfully, "submit" is merely a word to describe a cooperative spirit. I finally received an accurate understanding of God's design.

Fear of submitting to headship is the plan of the enemy to cause marriages and homes to be out of balance and out of order. God established order in everything He created. The family is no exception because marriage was His design from the beginning.

So, we should desire that our marriages reflect God's original design. Why would we want anything other than that? Why should we take issue with the way God designed the home and marriage to operate? The answer is that we should not!

We must move beyond the mental arguments and overcome this fear. We must encourage our husbands to be who God ordained them to be in our homes. These actions will cause us to experience peace in our homes and family. Order will always produce peace, safety, and tranquility.

If you want to experience the peace of God in your home, then allow your husband to take his role as the head, just as it was ordained and commanded in God's Word. Again, this does not mean a husband is to dominate; wives should cooperate and help him in his leadership role. This allows him the opportunity to be the leader God called and ordained him to be.

Headship Means Responsibility

For husbands, it must be understood that headship does not mean domination but rather taking responsibility. Far too many people define "headship" as a dictatorship. The husband is not to be authoritarian when taking his role as the head of the home. He should imitate Jesus and take responsibility for the decisions and atmosphere in the family.

The Bible tells us that just as Christ is head of the church, the husband is head of the home. If wives stand in opposition to this, we hinder our husbands from fulfilling the very command they are biblically given. Thereby, we are hindering their obedience to God's Word. We stand in the way of the highest call of husbands.

When we allow our husbands to take the headship role, it is his responsibility to example Jesus. We are not responsible for his actions, only our own. He must take spiritual responsibility to maintain proper order and lead by love. Understand that it is the husband's primary responsibility to set the tone or atmosphere within the home. Letting him take the lead does not make you unimportant or invisible; it covers you. Allow him the grace to be who God ordained him to be.

Do Not Blame

While it is the husband's responsibility to set the proper course in the family, it does not give wives the right to blame their husbands for anything that goes awry. Things happen—life happens. Sometimes, good people make wrong decisions. Just because something fails to go how we thought does not give us the right to blame and complain. On the contrary, it is our opportunity to be the helper God designed and assist in finding a solution.

Anyone and everyone can find something wrong, but can you be the encourager when things have an unexpected outcome? It is easy to sit in the scorner's seat, but can you stand as a support in difficult situations? Refuse to be one who finds fault and complains, rather be one who aids and assists.

Jesus led by example. Likewise, a husband should do the same in his household. Leadership should never be demonstrated with the attitude of "do as I say, not as I do." Every action and decision should be borne out of love and appreciation for one another. The simple principle of sowing and reaping will affect our marriage. If we desire respect in our home, then we respect our spouse. If we want to be loved, we give and demonstrate love. If we need grace, we give grace.

Arrange in Order

Let's look again at the word "**submit**"! It is the word that I had so much trouble with due to my incorrect understanding. I had observed people using this biblical command in the wrong way. Hence, I wanted no part of anything controlling and demeaning to the person doing the submitting. However, to submit is in the Bible, just like John 3:16 is there.

The apostle Paul directed wives to submit to their own husbands, as unto the Lord. The word "submit" is derived from two Greek words, the first being the word *hupo*, meaning under, and *tasso*, meaning to arrange in an orderly manner. Everything always works better when we do things according to the Word. Many women question why their homes are in turmoil or why their husbands avoid spending time with them while the wife constantly tries to take his position in the relationship. Things always work better when they are arranged properly in order.

Puzzle pieces are made to fit in specific places to create a beautiful picture. But, when pieces are forced into place, they will never complete the proper image. God wants your marriage to be a beautiful picture, not a broken mess. Therefore, we must position ourselves in the appropriate place. Only then can we see and experience the beauty God desires in our marriage and relationship.

Ladies, if you try to function in a place God has not designed you to function, you will constantly be frustrated. Allow your husband to be who God created him to be. Step out of the way and let him lead you as he follows Christ. You will live with so much more peace, and he will live with so much more confidence.

The Balance

Again, this does not mean that you lose your voice and influence. Nor does this mean that you are inferior to your husband. On the contrary, positioning yourself according to the biblical admonition produces a greater platform for your thoughts, opinions, and ideas. **It does not diminish your value; it elevates your worth.** When received, it causes the power struggle to cease and brings peace. After all, this is the way God designed our marriage to be. It was not intended to be a constant power struggle between two stubborn people but rather a place of mutual respect and honor for one another as we fulfill our roles together.

I would be negligent if I failed to emphasize that no spouse should ever submit to anything they are asked or told to do that is unbiblical. Nor should anyone ever submit to something that violates their conscience. We should never disobey God's Word or the voice of the Holy Spirit in the name of being submitted. All of us are, first and foremost, submitted to the Lord and His Word. That is why Paul said that wives are to submit to their own husbands "as unto the Lord."

All biblical commands are to be measured and balanced with other principles expressed in the Bible. There is never to be any sort of blind obedience to anyone's spouse; that would be bondage and unbiblical. Peter said, "We ought to obey God rather than men" (Acts 5:29). Never submit to anyone who asks you to do something sinful, unbiblical, unlawful, or unholy. Just say, "No!"

God's Perfect Plan

God's perfect will for our marriage is to allow our spouses to be who God designed them to be. Truthfully, most conflicts would be resolved if we just did this. Wives get in trouble when we attempt to take a relationship role where God never equipped us. It is impossible for either spouse to be anything other than their assigned role. A husband cannot be a wife or mother, and a wife cannot be a husband or father. Embracing this understanding alone will resolve many issues that arise.

Be confident in the role God designed for you. Be gracious and forgive often. Be a doer of the Word when it comes to your role as a husband or wife. This will create an atmosphere of heaven on earth in your marriage and home.

Ask Yourself

Here are some things to consider: Are you being a friend to your spouse or their corrector? Is the law of kindness regularly on your tongue? Do you compliment and encourage your spouse, or do you prefer to nag? Are you willing to take responsibility for your part in the marital relationship, or is it easier to blame your spouse for the failures? These questions demand us to take an honest look at what we are doing to determine if we are building up our home or harming it. ***Sheer commitment*** to doing the right thing will cause your marriage to live and thrive!

10

GET REAL

Let's get real about where we live or have lived at some point in time. Some people may be reluctant to admit it, but it is a place where many people dwell. It is a dangerous place to reside, yet so many people still choose to live there. It is the place called **comparison**.

Unfortunately, many marriages fail today because they constantly compare their marriage, spouse, children, and life to everyone else. It is a snare that can cause you to not appreciate who you are, who your spouse is, and what your marriage and life look like. This place will cause you to be dissatisfied while fantasizing about being someone else. It is a place of self-torment.

The apostle Paul warned against comparing yourself to others, calling it unwise. However, many do it every day in numerous areas of their lives. People may say, "*I'm not pretty enough. I'm not smart enough. My husband is not like hers. I don't have a college degree. I'm not a good cook. I'm not skinny enough. Our house is not big enough.*" The list goes on without end.

There is always something we can disdain about our own life. It can be our career, our house, our financial status, or just life in general if we look critically enough. Unfortunately, in today's world, we have every aid under the sun to help us compare and complain. We are baptized into a culture that constantly shouts that we are missing out.

Media Comparisons

In the world of television, internet, and social media of every type, we are bombarded with those who want to tell us everything they have done or can do. We are told how to be more beautiful by applying make-up in a certain way. We are instructed about the organization of every nook and cranny of our homes. There are even those who tell us how to have the best sex life ever.

If that is not enough, we have others who know how to raise perfect children and lose those unwanted pounds in days. Just scroll for one minute on your favorite social platform, and you will easily be mesmerized by someone who seems to be better, do better, or have better than you. It is an endless list of people with things we wish we had. So, this results in comparisons as we long to be like those observed on these platforms.

Comparison is an age-old problem that has been heightened by social media. However, we cannot allow ourselves to fall prey to the trap and get caught up in comparing who we are and what we have to others. Again, the Bible says doing that is **not** wise. So, we must break this pattern of comparing ourselves with others; it is key to having a strong and happy marriage.

Fearfully and Wonderfully Made

We must understand that everyone is created equal and beautiful in the sight of God. One of my favorite Scriptures is Psalms 139:14, "I will praise You, for I am fearfully and wonderfully made." God created you wonderfully! He can only create amazing things. Understand that when God created you, He knew precisely what He was doing, and you are made beautifully, just like the Scripture says. It's just that simple. We need to believe it and walk with our heads held up high, not in an arrogant way, but in a confident manner. When He created you, He broke the mold. It was not broken because He failed but because you were just that wonderful.

We cannot allow our lives to be controlled by comparing ourselves with the appearance or success of others. We merely need to be that wonderfully made person that our Father created us to be. Life is not a beauty pageant, a social status contest, an intelligence quest, or a parent of the year contest. Your life should be an "I will fulfill my purpose" quest.

If we always look outward at others, we will never see what God has placed within us. We must not pattern our life, marriage, or family after others who seem to have it all together. We should not attempt to emulate Hollywood actors, influencers on social sites, famous rock stars, worship leaders, or even our favorite pastors and ministers. They all have bad hair days, kids that scream, and even disagreements with their spouses. A perfectly painted picture is not always reality. So, refuse to compare your life with those who may possess a more visible platform.

Attitude of Gratitude

Constantly comparing yourself to the blessings you observe in others will cause you to be blind to the blessings you already possess. However, if we show gratitude, we will cease to compare and complain. Praise will always shift your mindset and silence the enemy in your life. Be thankful for who you are and the potential that is within you. Gratitude will change your disposition and shut down the thoughts and voices of comparison.

Some of you may have heard the old song by Lynn Anderson called "Rose Garden." The "hook" or most popular line in the song says, "I beg your pardon; I never promised you a rose garden. Along with the sunshine, there's gonna be a little rain sometimes." This is what we call life. We live and learn. We don't quit; we continue to run the race with the understanding that with God, all things are possible. We know that with Him by our side, we cannot fail. We may have a little rain on some days, but the sun will shine again. Understand this: It takes both the rain and the sunshine to produce beautiful roses. Think about it!

We all have situations that we face. Because of living in a fallen world, we all experience bad days and difficult situations. All of us have bad hair and bad breath when we wake up in the morning. Now, think about this: Your favorite social media influencer experiences the same things you do. Their kids cry, spit up, and have accidents, too! The fact is the superhuman life that you are trying to live does not exist. We must not get so caught up in the lives of others that we forget to live ours to the fullest.

My Own Battle

Many years ago, when our children were young, we traveled ministering throughout the United States and Canada. For about a decade, we were on the road almost as much as at home. We were afforded the opportunity to experience and see things that some have never and will never be able to encounter. Looking back now, I can see how blessed we were. However, I did not always display the most appreciative attitude.

Traveling with three small children in a van across the country was difficult. We never knew what hotel we might land in for the night or if there would even be enough beds for our family of five. Unfortunately, the accommodations were insufficient and cramped for us much of the time. We would travel for hours upon hours and miles upon miles to get from meeting to meeting. Our children were well-behaved troupers. Many times, they behaved better than I did. Instead of seeing and appreciating the fact that we were able to experience things that most families don't have the opportunity to do, I complained and compared my life to others.

Looking back, I find myself grateful for the long van rides and the time spent together as a family. But most of all, I see God's plan for our family and for my husband's voice to mold them into who they are in ministry today. We all laugh that they could preach his sermons and tell his stories word-for-word even still today. What a blessing to have both of our voices in their lives.

To those looking at us, they might say that we had it "made in the shade." We possessed the opportunity to travel the United States with our kids. It was like being on constant vacation, or so it appeared. However, it was not all sunshine and butterflies. We had various meltdowns, times our kids slept in bathtubs or recliners, and at least one child was in bed with us. It was difficult. However, life is full of both challenging and rewarding things, all in the same box. What you see and experience are determined more by your perspective and how you respond to what you encounter.

What Do You See?

Far too often, we peer into the lives of others and see what we want to see. We see a husband who dotes over his wife, but we fail to see their argument yesterday over something that really did not matter in the grand scheme. We see the woman with the perfect body, but we do not see the pain in her eyes because she was unable to have children, thus giving her that untouched figure. We see the perfect little family traveling the country, seeing all the sights, but not the bathtub beds or the roach motels! We see exactly what we want to see.

Comparing our lives with others can cause the things we once loved about our spouse to become major irritants. If we become obsessed with other people's marriages and families while refusing to see and appreciate our own, we will despise every good thing about our own relationship and family. We will attempt to make our spouse into someone or something different instead of appreciating everything we once loved so much about them.

What happened to the person with whom you fell in love? Did they change, or did you change? Are your comparisons driving a wedge and painting a picture of an alternate reality? Are you allowing your spouse to be who God called them to be, or are you trying to remake them into something and someone else? Perhaps you are looking at the wrong picture.

Do You Remember?

Do you remember when your spouse was your dream? They were everything you wanted and needed! He was your Mr. Right and could do nothing wrong. What happened to that person? What happened to you? We travel down a road of fault-finding, which leads to disappointment. This is where comparisons lead us.

We must not let comparisons change the way we view our spouse. After all, we could not live without them at one time. If we are not careful, we will get caught up in unrealistic expectations and focus on our spouse's shortcomings instead of all the strengths they possess.

Everything you see and hear about the person you follow on Facebook®, Instagram®, YouTube®, or at your place of employment only represents part of their story that they allow you to see and hear. The truth is that we are all human. We all have flaws and strengths. Focus on the strengths and work on the weaknesses in your life. Stop believing you would be better off in a different relationship or that your spouse would be better off if they had only married someone else.

There have been times I struggled with my own insecurities and thought that Robert, my husband, would have been much better off without me. I let my insecurities and self-pity take me down a road that was neither true nor healthy for our relationship. The truth is that I need him, and he needs me. He has strengths that I need, and I have strengths he needs.

We complete each other. The enemy wants nothing more than to lead you down the road of insufficiency in your marriage. Refuse to allow him to take you on that journey. Resist every lie the enemy has spoken about you and your spouse. God has joined you together, and you are the perfect team!

The Trial of My Faith

When Robert and I were young, at the beginning of our ministry, he was the worship pastor at a local church. We served under a young pastor who was demanding and driven. His priorities were God, your ministry, and then your family. We never bought into that train of thought but honored and respected him even though we disagreed with placing ministry above family. However, since that pastor held to this perspective, we kept an intense schedule. Ministry and success were his primary focus. It was a challenging season in our lives and taxing on our relationship.

It appeared that this pastor and his wife had the perfect marriage. They knew all the right people, wore nice clothes, and had everything a young married couple could hope for. I looked up to them and esteemed them highly. They appeared to be successful, and everyone loved them. He could preach a powerful message, and so could his wife. They were a true power couple, or so it appeared.

One day, my husband returned home after meeting with the pastor, and Robert shared what they discussed with me. I was shocked and hurt, to say the least, when told I had been one of the topics of conversation that day.

My World Was Rocked to the Core

If you recall, I previously discussed how I never felt called to the ministry but promised to support Robert and follow him to the ends of the earth and back. I meant every word and believed with all my heart that I had proved it in all my actions. I supported his every endeavor and was continuously involved in the church, singing on the worship team, keeping nursery, and always being present. So, I was overwhelmingly shocked when Robert told me that our pastor said, "As long as you are married to Stacey, you will go nowhere in ministry!"

This conversation rocked me to the core. Being young and insecure, I struggled with the idea that I was insufficient. I had not gone to ministry college or any college; we married right out of high school. I seemingly had no real talents to offer as far as ministry went. The pastor's statement confirmed what I had already told myself many times: Robert should have chosen someone else to marry. More than that, hearing that my pastor said something like this to my husband sent me into a tailspin that took me years to recover. You may ask why he shared the pastor's comment with me. He did it because we pledged to one another from day one of our marriage that we would not keep any secrets.

Robert reassured me of his love, and we kept doing what we knew was right. I tried not to let it affect me, but it did! I had to be healed of the opinions of others. I had to understand that Robert loved me, and I was just what he needed; likewise, he was exactly what I needed. Together, we could and would do what God planned for us, and we would be successful.

Be Secure in Who You Are

The enemy set me up! Satan works by using people who unknowingly reinforce your ungodly beliefs. People will always have opinions about you, but what really matters is that you are secure in your relationship with the Lord and who you are in Christ. You must also be secure in the relationship with your spouse. Refuse to allow the opinions of others to cause you to second guess your marriage. Remember what the Bible says, "What God has joined together, let not man separate" (Matthew 19:6). It does not matter what others think or say. Be confident and committed to being better together. Keep doing what you know to do, and don't let people's opinions or words stop you from running together. You must understand that others won't have to answer for what God has called you to do, but you will. So, keep pressing toward the prize of the high calling in Christ Jesus.

Robert and I have now celebrated over forty years of marriage and ministry. We pastored a thriving church for over twenty-five years, which we now oversee. We provide spiritual oversight for numerous ministers and churches. Together, we raised three beautiful children who are all serving the Lord in ministry today. It has been proven that we are better together. Thank you, Jesus!

Unfortunately, we witnessed our former pastor who made that unbelievable statement to my husband all those years ago have several failed marriages and relationships. Sadly, he was away from the Lord at one point. More recently, his relationship with the Lord has been restored. Praise the Lord!

It is crucial to refuse to be influenced by what others say about your marriage and family. We prioritized our relationship and refused to become bitter because of the opinions of others. Our focus was maintained as we refused to allow the comparison of others to dictate our marriage and home.

I encourage you to refuse to let others affect what you believe about yourself: who you are and who you can be. Do not put people on a pedestal while putting yourself in a pit. Do not count yourself and your marriage out because another marriage looks different and possibly appears better than yours. Looks can be deceiving. Just be faithful to be the best that you can be. The bottom line is to give your all to your spouse, marriage, and family. Model your marriage after God's design rather than something you see on television or social media. Love your spouse, and remember what captured your heart at the beginning of your relationship.

No Secrets

It is essential for couples to be honest and real with each other. They must learn to be transparent and have no secrets. If there is anything that you conceal from your spouse, it is an area that the devil will invade to bring havoc. Secrets open the door to sin and destruction. For that reason, spouses must practice transparency in their relationship.

We live in an internet and social media-driven world. Most everyone I know uses the internet to some degree or another. Many occupations utilize social media outlets. Unfortunately, these connections and relationships made online can result in inappropriate relationships and behaviors.

I personally know people who divorced because their spouse rekindled a previous relationship with a high school flame that resulted in adultery. It started with them innocently chatting online. Then it graduated to them sending pictures to each other. The next thing you know, they were exchanging photos of their private body parts. Ultimately, they arranged a place to meet for illicit sex.

These things happen partly because secrets are kept, accompanied by no accountability. These actions eliminate transparency within the marital relationship. Spouses become two ships passing in the night that know nothing concerning their partner's life. He does his thing, and she does hers. They do things and keep secrets.

Have Nothing to Hide

My husband can access my phone, social media page, or computer whenever he desires. He knows my passwords and can examine any of my internet history. The same goes for his phone and other electronic devices; I have free reign to look at them any time. We have nothing to hide because we are transparent with one another. It is unwise to hide things from your spouse.

If a person will not allow their spouse to examine their phone, then they are hiding something sinful. If they refuse to let their spouse on their computer or tablet, then they are hiding something unholy. Transparency is necessary for husbands and wives to embrace and practice.

The greatest thing that happens when couples do this is accountability is afforded. The first person that anyone should be accountable to is their spouse. Forget being accountable to a friend at work if you are not firstly accountable to your spouse. A friend will let you slide and honor the excuses you make; your spouse will not. They will hold your feet to the fire, which is what needs to happen in these types of situations. They will warn you at the sight of danger, while others will not be so quick to do so.

Naked Before Each Other

When God created Adam and Eve, He placed them in the Garden of Eden naked. They were bare before each other. This is a picture of how we must be with our spouse. Our life stands open and bare before them; we hide nothing. This is how a God-ordained marriage should be. He did not intend for the man and woman to hide things from one another.

We must get real with our spouse. There needs to be a willingness to lay everything out in the open. Transparency will unlock greater intimacy and keep the devil out of your relationship. Be open and honest; it will cause great dividends to be reaped within your marriage and home.

Ask Yourself

Answer these questions honestly: Do you compare yourself, your spouse, or your marriage with others? Are media and television shaping what you believe to be the perfect relationship? What voices are you listening to, and is it possible they are painting an incorrect picture in your mind? Are you open and honest with your spouse about everything in your life and marriage? All of us need to get real with our partners. ***Sheer commitment*** to live openly and honestly before God and one another is the pathway to life and freedom.

11

No Escape & Murder Is Not an Option

Every marriage has its ups and downs—good times and challenging times. It is how we navigate those challenging times that is so important. Life is easy when everything is coming up roses, but that is not the reality in which we live. It is effortless to love when there is no trouble, and your spouse agrees with everything you say and do. However, I know from experience this is not the way life goes.

The truth is that when two people come together and become one flesh, they do not automatically and magically agree in every situation and circumstance. It is usually rare that they see eye-to-eye on things. Becoming one flesh is a process of maturing together—bending and molding. Both parties must exercise grace and understanding while maintaining flexibility, not rigidity. Remember, flexible things bend and stay together, whereas rigid things break and fall to pieces.

There is a place in the wedding ceremony my husband has performed numerous times where he makes this statement, "Marriage is a lifetime commitment. It is 'til death do you part, and murder is not an option." Everyone usually responds with a laugh. The statement is meant to bring some levity to a serious statement, but at the same time, it makes a profound mark in the hearts and minds of people.

Modern Society

Sadly, in today's society, marriage vows are taken so lightly and easily broken. It is as if a couple is simply repeating words to one another on a beautiful fairytale day without realizing the weight of those words. Many seem to go through the actions without understanding the covenant made to one another. Again, they are repeating mere words uttered on their fairytale day with no awareness about the gravity of their commitment.

When we view marriage as a single day rather than a lifetime, we will always feel we have an escape hatch. If we fail to understand the power of covenant and the gravity of the vows exchanged, we will never fully give ourselves to one another.

The Bible declares that people perish for a lack of knowledge. Many marriages suffer and then end needlessly in divorce due to a lack of understanding. They fail to gain the necessary insight that causes their fairytale day to become their forever-love story.

The "Me First" Culture

We live in a "me first" culture. This influence causes many marriages to suffer because spouses feel justified in being self-centered. This self-absorbed attitude causes many to give up on their relationships when it becomes apparent that work and sacrifice are needed. When the emotions and feelings they had on their wedding day are no longer present, they are ready to quit.

Unfortunately, divorce is at an all-time high for both believers and unbelievers. At the same time, more marriage books and videos are available than ever before. Knowledge is available, but many do not seek it. Instead, they rely on the temporary emotions of the moment to take them through. Unfortunately, they end up disappointed. Feelings are fleeting and will not always be present. Your marriage must be established on a solid foundation, beginning with commitment and understanding.

There was a day when people understood the gravity of their wedding vows. In our self-absorbed society, perhaps vows would sound more like this: "*As long as you make me feel good about myself and never disagree with me… As long as you are not demanding of my time and resources… As long as your expectations of me are acceptable to me… As long as nobody better comes along.*" Even though no one actually says those things, it is often what is lived out.

It's Not About You; It's About Us

Many husbands and wives have no understanding of the kind of commitment that says, "*I'm here come hell or high water. No matter what we have to face, we will face it together!*" This is the one-flesh attitude that says, "*Wherever you go, I'll go.*" It is crucial to put yourself aside if you desire to have a great marriage. The idea that it is all about you and your desires must go out the window. Once you are married, it's not about you; it's about us!

When you make a vow, you should fully understand the words you are speaking and the commitment you are making to one another. We need to view this as more than words; it is a spiritual contract—a heavenly covenant. This kind of commitment chooses to believe the best of our spouse and always puts each other first.

Marriage is a promise you should fulfill and fully exercise daily for a lifetime. Regardless of what life throws your way, you choose to remain constant with your spouse. This is the only way to have a marriage that will be sustained and even flourish in the different seasons of life that you experience together. That is the ***sheer commitment*** kind of promise that keeps you steady when things seem unstable.

An Imperfect Marriage Doesn't Mean Divorce

Marriage is not always perfect because people are not perfect. No matter how great they are, every person alive has said or done things that knowingly or unknowingly hurt someone they love. This is called life. Welcome to Earth. The truth is that we all have been guilty of being the person who hurt someone we love or the person hurt by someone we love. We must choose to exercise love and grace in these situations.

An imperfect marriage with two imperfect people does not mean you should divorce one another to find another imperfect person and have another imperfect marriage. We all go through days and sometimes weeks of difficulty, but quitting is not the solution. We must learn to navigate through the rough seasons of our relationship.

Learning to be longsuffering should be our goal. We can be full of grace, exercise understanding, and enact forgiveness. As we are being perfected and conformed to the image of Christ, we must grow together. We do not suddenly arrive at a state of spiritual maturity upon saying, "I do." Do not give up on your spouse just because they have yet to arrive at the place of perfection. Remember, you are not there, either. Think about it!

What if everyone who made a covenant and spoke vows of commitment and lasting love to one another decided to honor those vows? What if divorce was not an option? What if we decided to break the mold and take the "d" word off the table? What if we did not have an escape hatch that was so easily accessible? I believe things would be much different.

Divorce is Easy; Marriage is Work

Divorce has become the easy road out of a marriage. We allow ourselves to become offended and eventually bitter toward our forever-love. Forgetting all their good attributes that were once so attractive to us prompts us to villainize them for the hurt they caused. When we do this, we open the door for the enemy to wreak havoc within our marriage. Satan will always tell you to take what seems to be the easy way out, that being divorce. The enemy of our soul, satan, is the one who promotes separation among relationships, while Jesus came to bring reconciliation.

Divorce today has become common and easy. Unfortunately, few people feel any remorse for giving up on their covenantal relationship. The Bible says, "What therefore God has joined together, let no man separate (Matthew 19:6; NASB)." However, people all over the world separate and give up instead of doing whatever it takes to make it work.

Marriage is no walk in the park. It takes effort. It takes dying to self and allowing your spouse's needs to be your first priority.

A successful marriage requires that you labor to see it succeed. It does not happen solely because you have butterflies in your stomach on your wedding day. Success happens because of diligence and faithfulness in doing the necessary work.

Remove Divorce from Your Vocabulary

Have you ever noticed that the more you do or say something, the easier it gets? This is how we develop habits, both good and bad. We were created this way, and it is human nature. Take, for example, learning to ride a bike. The more you ride, the more proficient you become. At first, it is not easy, but the more you do it, the easier it gets. Our conversation is much the same. The more we use words, good or bad, the more natural they become part of our vocabulary until we use them without thought in given situations.

Divorce is one of those words we should never allow to become part of our speech. For the sake of your marriage, take the word "divorce" off the table. We must refuse to let it enter our vocabulary. It must be deemed a word of profanity. It must be seen as an enemy of your marital relationship, just as sickness is an enemy of your body.

During the early years of our marriage, we did not have this understanding. Therefore, it was a word used during conflict because of past hurts. It was a weapon that we would pull out of our arsenal designed to hurt one another and attempt to gain the upper hand. Little did we know that it was really the enemy reinforcing insecurities that were present and driving a wedge of doubt and mistrust between two people who truly loved each other.

I remember many days and nights of raised voices and cruel words spoken as shields to counter attacks. We said things to each other in our youthful ignorance and spiritual immaturity that hurt one another. We must remember that our words have the power to curse and the power to bless. Every word spoken in anger, retaliation, or spite creates wounds that must be healed. Unfortunately, this happened often and became a normal defense tactic in our relationship. The word "divorce" became much too common in our vocabulary. The more we said it, the easier the idea became.

Thank God for His grace and mercy and that we both were just hardheaded enough to not give up. We at least had the mentality that we were not quitters; we would not become another statistic. Our heart conviction was that we were to be married forever. However, the words sown were words of hurt, and we needed healing.

The Promise—No More "D" Word

Healing began with a promise we made to each other not to use the "d" word. Divorce would not be an option for us. No matter how heated or upset we were, we would not let that word continue to be spoken in our home. What we allowed to become common had to be arrested and removed from our mouths. We could not allow it to be a dart thrown to hurt each other. Fully embracing our covenant allowed us to resolve the fact that divorce was not in the equation. We had to change our vocabulary to heal what we had damaged with our fleshly language. It is important to speak words that reinforce our marriage vows rather than ones that cause critical damage and possible destruction.

The truth is you can leave and go somewhere else, but you can never escape yourself. Wherever you go, you will still be there. Pastoring has permitted us to peer into the lives of many relationships. We have seen those who were broken and ready to call it quits. Many of them put in the work and experienced complete restoration and healing. From that, we have seen them thrive and have what they call "a marriage better than before."

However, we have also witnessed the ones who would not listen, couples who would not look introspectively, and those who viewed their spouse as the problem. Sadly, their marriages faltered and failed. The enemy had convinced them the problems in their marriage had nothing to do with them. All the pain and dissatisfaction they experienced was their spouse's fault. They were unwilling to entertain the thought that both spouses play a role in the breakdown of a marital relationship. These are the things that place people on the road of separation.

If He Would Only...

I recall one particular situation where the wife was upset and wanted to point out all her husband's faults. She constantly brought up his past shortcomings. As we spoke, we heard, "he doesn't," and "if he would only." She failed to take responsibility for anything. It was obvious that she wanted out of the relationship and was unwilling to see or hear anything to the contrary. No number of apologies from her husband was going to change her mind. She was fully determined to end the marriage, and she eventually did.

This woman allowed someone other than her husband—another man—to become the priority in her life. She did what no married person should ever do; she permitted another to become the love of her life and confidant. She had an adulterous relationship and justified it by focusing on all her husband's faults and shortcomings instead of facing her own sin.

The Grass Is Not Greener

You may have heard the analogy, "The grass is always greener on the other side." This young wife believed that anecdote as she looked across the fence into another man's field. Not only did she look, but she began to play there. Unfortunately, this broke her covenant and destroyed her marriage and children and also the wife and children of the man with whom she was having the affair.

As we watched this happen, it saddened our hearts deeply. This young lady had so much potential with her husband and children. It was wasted because what seemed greener was only destructive. She lied to herself and those she loved, causing turmoil that her children had to endure due to her choices. Many lives were altered forever due to her decision to break covenant and look elsewhere. Listen to me: It is just not worth it!

Don't believe the lie that "the grass is always greener on the other side." Instead, get to work and put in the extra time and energy to fertilize the place you have chosen to call home. Your own spouse and family will appreciate it and love you for it.

I have often wondered why people are so in love one day and then despise each other the next. We allow little things to creep in; before we know it, we question our choices. Think about this: You chose your spouse; no one required you to marry them. To question your choice is to doubt your judgment. If someone doubts their judgment, why not doubt the decision to divorce? The best choice is to doubt divorce. Think about it!

Look In the Mirror

What if we determine within ourselves that we made the right choice and focused on ourselves to become the right person instead of looking to our spouse to be the right person? It is easy to get caught in the trap of fault-finding others and never look at where we fall short. We always want to play the blame game when we are unhappy in our relationships. The enemy attempts to get you into a vicious cycle that will break down even the best relationships. This behavior needs to be arrested and halted.

What if we put as much focus on being the right person as finding the right person? What if we ask the Holy Spirit to bring to light the things in us that are not like Him? What if we give Him permission to transform us into His image and likeness? Think of the transformation that this would bring to your relationship. It would stop the constant questioning of whether we found the right person because we are busy becoming the right person.

We must learn to deal with irritating things that get on our nerves, things that make us boil, and things that make us doubt our commitment. If we fail to do so, frustrations will turn to disdain, and we will unknowingly open the door for the enemy in our marriage. Unresolved conflict will become mountains that cause separation, seemingly insurmountable and impossible to traverse.

I am sure you have heard the adage, "They made a mountain out of a molehill." Many times, that is exactly what we do. We allow slight differences to become major points of separation in our relationship. We let the little things fester into major things or, as they call them in divorce proceedings, "irreconcilable differences." Your marriage is the most important place to learn and enact conflict resolution. We must learn not to sweat the small stuff and resolve the major things with a proper attitude and perspective.

Simple Conflict Resolution

The first thing that I believe will help resolve conflict in your marriage and home is to simply be quiet and listen. Being quick to hear and slow to speak is crucial in the marriage relationship.

To effectively resolve conflict that may occur in your relationship, it is wise to not discuss things in a heated moment. No one ever says things when they are angry that they relish later. The apostle James said, "No man can tame the tongue. It is an unruly evil, full of deadly poison" (James 3:8). This means that nothing good will happen if you open your mouth when you are angry or upset. You will say things for which you have to apologize later. So, if you are heated, mad, or know you are about to say something you shouldn't say, just zip it!

Controlling your tongue is key to bringing resolution to conflict. Saying the right thing can bring peace, whereas saying the wrong thing can heighten contention. Most verbal fights within marriages could be eliminated if spouses controlled their tongues and bathed their words with love rather than speaking from an angry heart.

Learn to Listen

Learning to listen is vital in conflict resolution. You need to listen, especially when you think you need to be heard. Listen to the Holy Spirit and not your emotions. Listen to your spouse rather than the mental arguments formed in moments of disagreement. If we let our emotions speak in times of conflict, we will most certainly sin. In the abundance of words, sin will surely abound (Proverbs 10:19).

For some people, listening comes easy. If that is you, congratulations! Unfortunately, listening never came easy for me. I was the queen of interrupting and defending myself before truly hearing my husband. I did not want to listen to him; I wanted him to hear me. I operated in a manner that only stoked the flame of contention rather than resolved the issue.

There is an old cliche, "If you want to be heard, then learn to listen." We often had long discussions and conversations about situations that could have been resolved quickly. However, it became an extreme and monumental issue solely because I was too busy speaking my mind. I did not take the time to listen to him. Once I learned how to truly listen, I stopped being defensive of my position and ceased striving to prove I was right. Most of the time, we were already on the same page the entire time.

Could a listening ear be all it takes to resolve a situation? The apostle James wrote, "So then, my beloved brethren, let every man [and maybe especially myself] be swift to hear, slow to speak, slow to wrath; for the wrath of man does not produce the righteousness of God" (James 1:19-20, emphasis added). Many of our conflicts could be resolved if we just stopped talking and started listening.

Work Like a Team

In sports, teams will lose if they argue and fight with one another during a game. Screaming and yelling at your teammate only shows weakness and gives the opponent the upper hand. No one can be heard, no plan can be enacted, and no progress can be made in the middle of contention.

To avoid these volatile situations, teams have a coach to whom they listen. He brings the team together for one goal and one purpose: to work together for the betterment of the team and achieve its goals, which is to beat their opponent and win the game.

We likewise have a coach to whom we should listen, the Holy Spirit. If we listen to the Lord and our spouse, we will experience a "WIN" in our marriage. When we choose to see our spouse as our teammate, it allows them to shine in the strengths they possess, and our relationship is reinforced. We are empowered to love "for better or worse, in sickness and in health, 'til death do us part," and murder will never be an option.

Choose to take divorce off the table. Take the "d" word out of your vocabulary. Leaving our spouse is not an option that we are willing to accept. We should not attempt to escape our marriage but work to make it the best relationship we have on earth. Always remember that the strength of your relationship is not determined by the total absence of conflict but rather by remaining together and united in the midst of it.

Ask Yourself

Ask yourself these questions and then take the appropriate action: Is divorce something you think about and consider? Does conflict within your marriage cause you to want to escape? What can you do to run to your spouse rather than run away from them? Will you take "divorce" off the table and out of your vocabulary? These are introspective issues that need to be addressed by everyone. I encourage you to make a ***sheer commitment*** that you are in your marriage for the long haul, and nothing can separate you.

12

OUCH! THAT HURTS

> Let your speech always be with grace, seasoned with salt, that you may know how you ought to answer each one (Colossians 4:6) .

This is such a beautiful Scripture that we should live by daily in everything we say. However, at times, I found myself not adhering to the words Paul so skillfully wrote. I have said hurtful, spiteful, and just mean things at times. These things were said not only to my spouse but others that I love, as well. Likewise, I have been the recipient of the same.

I do not believe anyone intentionally wants to hurt those they love the most. No one sets out to tear down the person closer to them than any other human being. Yet, our spouse can become the target of our frustrations, anger, moodiness, bad hair days, and any other negative emotions.

If things are not going well or going the way we desire, then many times, our spouse becomes the bullseye of our poor attitude and frustrations. Our expressions of disdain for our situation or circumstance are aimed at them, even though they did nothing to contribute to it. Unfortunately, we open our mouths, and hurtful words begin to fly. Unfortunately, in these moments, we exalt our own feelings above our spouse's.

In this chapter, I want to share with you my real-life adventure of learning, of which I am in a constant state, to say things with grace and not out of anger or frustration. When I failed, I was quick to apologize and ask for forgiveness. I want to share how learning to be open to hearing and slow to defend my actions and speech made a difference in our spousal relationship.

I have been in this process for over sixty years and have yet to perfect everything. However, I have learned many lessons through my journey and will learn more in the future. The Bible declares that we are being conformed to the image of Christ. This means we are all in a process of spiritual growth and maturity, and it will continue until we leave this earth.

Seasoned with Grace

Paul said that our conversation is to be seasoned with grace. The ***Strong's Exhaustive Concordance*** definition of "grace" is the divine influence upon the heart that is then reflected within the life. This is literally God's divine empowerment to live above sin. We could also say it like this, "*God gives us the divine power to control our tongue and speak words that are life-giving, not life-sucking!*" How many times have you been in a conversation that "went south" quickly just because someone began to gripe, complain, or blame the other person? That is a prime example of not allowing conversation to be seasoned with grace.

When we fail to think before we speak and understand that our situation is temporary, we will speak out of our circumstances and not out of grace and gratitude. We react irrationally when we fail to take a moment, breathe, and realize how much God has blessed us.

I had to practice these actions while writing this book. My day had been filled with typing as I put my thoughts into words. My husband decided to collaborate with me and help edit as I was writing. He attempted to upload all I had written to the "cloud" to work on it together. In the process, he was given a dreadful upload error message. Unfortunately, this resulted in the loss of approximately four thousand words (an entire chapter) that I had diligently written.

My first response could have been anger, blame, or shame. However, I chose a different response because it was the right thing to do, and I had to live what I was writing. God has a real sense of humor. Knowing that this was nothing more than an error that could not be helped, I attempted to respond with grace. I held my tongue and decided to make sure he knew it was ok.

Robert felt so badly that this had happened. He repeatedly apologized because he knew how much I had worked on writing those words. I told him countless times that it would be all right because I knew he felt terrible, and it was beyond his control. Even though composition writing never came easy for me, I recognized that I was being tested to act upon my own words of wisdom. I had to choose to be kind.

Real-Life Lessons

Robert was only attempting to assist me when this happened. I continued to reassure him that I would rewrite it, and the chapter would be better the second time. Thus, this story was born. It was a lesson I had to live out. Life offers opportunities to learn and improve, and I was given one immediately. I could have failed, but I chose to remain calm and let God use it to make me better. I allowed my conversation to be seasoned with grace.

For those of you who know me, it was difficult for me to respond in this manner. My usual response would be to freak out like my life had just ended. It would have been one of anger mixed with much drama. Yes! I can be quite dramatic. However, in that situation, I chose grace!

I chose to reassure him and not get caught up in "me" and "my" feelings. I made sure he knew that I understood his action was unintentional. After all, he is my biggest cheerleader and best friend. I stopped and told myself to calm down because I know him and that his heart is to help me. I am confident he cares about me and the marriages this book will help. I know he would never do anything to sabotage me. I had to stop, not be reactionary, take a breath, consider my response, and not sin with my words or actions.

Redefine Sin

Many times, we do not consider what we speak to our spouse in anger to be a sin. We tell ourselves that it is ok because we love each other. Why would we even consider hurting those we love with words that we know will do nothing but drive a wedge and cause hurt and mistrust? Sin is sin and cannot be justified. The enemy's plan is to divide, and if he can cause us to be comfortable with words of accusation, shame, and blame, then he can get a foothold in our relationship. If satan can cause us to sin against each other with our words, we open the door to him.

We must guard our mouths so division does not happen. Choose to believe the best. In difficult and disappointing situations, believe God will use it for our good. He can turn things around in our lives if we just believe Him and refuse to sin with our words.

Have you ever heard the saying, "It's not what you say, but how you say it?" Many arguments and hurt feelings could be avoided if we considered not only our choice of words but also our body language and tone before we speak. Often, we use our tongues to defend and offend instead of building and improving a situation. It is so easy to fall into the trap of self-preservation and forget that we should think before we speak. It is easy to feel like life is all about "me" and forget that it is about you as a couple—a healthy, happy marriage and sharing life together.

It's Not What You Say, but How You Say It

I remember one Sunday morning early in our marriage when we were running a little late for church. Robert was quite agitated that I was not moving as quickly as he thought I should. The fact was, I was feeling quite insecure about my appearance that morning. My hair was not cooperating, I felt as though my choice of clothing was less than adequate, and I was just having an all-around rough morning. All the while, Robert was pacing the floor, more concerned about being tardy than my morning issues.

Hoping to get some positive affirmation from him, I asked, "How do I look?" His response was, "FINE; let's go!" He said the right words but in the wrong manner. I heard this: "*We are late, and you are only making matters worse! Get your butt out the door and in the car. I don't care what you look like or how you feel.*" I did not hear him say, "*Baby, you look amazing! You are always beautiful to me. Are you ready to go? We are running a little behind this morning."*

As you can imagine, the way he responded led to further delays as tears ran down my face, causing my make-up to run and clothing decisions to be questioned. He legitimately needed to get to the church, but his hurriedness caused him to say something in such a way that hurt my feelings. It wasn't what he said but how he said it. This lesson has stuck with both of us to this day.

Tasty Conversation

In the beginning Scripture of this chapter, we read that Paul also instructed that our words should be "seasoned with salt." Have you ever eaten unseasoned food? It's pretty awful and "hard to swallow." When we refuse to season our words before speaking them, the recipient may have difficulty swallowing them. A great rule to live by is this: Would I like to be spoken to in the way I am speaking?

I am sure many of the things that we deal out, we could never take. Yet, we feel justified in "blessing" others with our bad attitudes and hateful words. This, my friend, is not the way to "win friends and influence people." It is certainly not the way to win the heart of your spouse. On the contrary, this is surely the way to cause strife and contention in your relationship. If you wish to be given grace, you should be a giver of the same. You will never receive what you are unwilling to give.

We all love the principle of seedtime and harvest when it comes to money and material things. However, we must understand that this principle works in every area of our lives, including our conversation and speech. The Bible says, "Whatever a man sows, that he will also reap" (Galatians 6:7). If we sow words of anger and bitterness, this is what we will reap. However, if we sow words of love, compassion, and appreciation, then that is what we will reap.

We should understand that the principles of the Word work all the time in every arena of life. Whatever we sow, we will reap. I would rather be the beneficiary of kindness rather than bitterness. Therefore, that is the seed I must sow.

Great Relationships Have Great Communication

Every great relationship is constructed upon great communication—the kind that uses words to build and does not tear down. Excellent communication speaks to potential in a kind, loving way and gives grace when needed while always preferring the other person.

One of the keys to having a great marriage is proper respect with words of kindness and grace rather than those of justification, retaliation, and anger. I am sure that we have all done or said things that have not been pleasant or uplifting to our spouse. We all fail at times. However, failure is not a reason to continue in a pattern of self-destruction; instead, it is an opportunity to apologize and do better.

It is important that we put a watch over our mouths so we do not sin (Psalm 141:3). Failure to do so will bring chaos and destruction. If we want our marriage to succeed, we must allow the Lord to deal with any pride in our hearts. It takes humility to admit we are wrong. It takes humility to apologize and accept fault. Saying that you are sorry is not a sign of weakness but rather a sign of great strength and love. If you never feel you must apologize, you probably need to address the pride in your heart.

> Sin is on their lips; all their words are sinful; may they be caught in their pride! (Psalm 59:12, GNT).

Someone once said, "Love is never having to say you are sorry." I vehemently disagree. Love is quick to repent and say you are sorry. Love will apologize even for the smallest things that were not done intentionally. Apologies are in the vocabulary of the language of love.

Proverbs 11:2 declares, "When pride comes in, then disgrace but with humility comes wisdom" (NIV). It is always better to walk in humility because wisdom will follow. My husband always says, "It is better to be reconciled than be right!" Many possess the philosophy of arguing until they win, but this is no way to live or have a healthy marriage. If you are wrong, admit it, apologize, and ask for forgiveness. Reconciliation is always better. Love can grow in a place where humility and grace flow.

Here are some principles for effective communication within your marriage and home:

Principle 1—Put Down Your Dukes

> Righteous people speak wisdom, but the tongue that speaks evil will be stopped. Righteous people know the kind thing to say, but the wicked are always saying things that hurt (Proverbs 10:31-32, GNT).

Wisdom always chooses words that will build up rather than tear down. It is never wise to take a defensive posture against your spouse as it will cause you to hear incorrectly and feel the need to defend and accuse. Remember, you are in this together; your spouse is not your enemy. On the contrary, they are your greatest asset against the enemy. Always let wisdom be your guide and kindness the rule by which you communicate.

My husband and I have had more than our fair share of disagreements, and they are never easy. We always see things from a different perspective. However, we must understand that this does not make either of us the enemy; it simply means we have different ideas and thoughts. Many arguments simply ensue because one person does not think like the other. When this happens, some people will belittle and accuse their spouse. Accusations will only heighten disagreements and cause hurtful things to be said.

I know from personal experience, and I am sure you will agree, that most arguments would cease if we refuse to be defensive and demand our own way. My husband and I had disagreements and arguments for hours simply because we were defensive in our positions. What began as a conversation became a major hurdle because one or both of us became defensive in our attitudes and words. After all the dust settled, we could not even remember what or how the disagreement started.

Recall that Proverbs tells us that righteous people speak wisdom, but wicked people are always saying hurtful things. How righteous are you when disagreements arise? Are you one who is throwing words like arrows to hurt your spouse, or are you considering what you say by using the filter of wisdom? Think about it!

The Boxing Match

Imagine for a minute a boxing match with two people poised to win a fight. This is how we often view our spouse—as our opponent instead of our teammate. Now, think about your life and your approach to disagreements and arguments. Are you in it to be declared the winner, or are you in it to find a resolution? Are you in it to be proclaimed as right, or are you truly seeking to find a place of agreement and peace? With a competitive disposition, even if you win, you lose. If you win and your spouse loses, you both end up defeated.

In marriage, we are often like two opponents wearing boxing gloves of hurtful words. We begin hurling our gloves of accusation. The harder they hit us, the harder we hit back. It becomes a vicious cycle that is unhealthy for the relationship and will never resolve any situation.

Our human nature teaches us that when hit, we hit back. Our goal becomes winning at all costs. If we operate in this manner within our marriage, it is a set-up for disaster and disappointment. However, if we put down our dukes, return to our perspective corners, allow the Holy Spirit (our coach) to administer healing to the hurt, and allow His voice to give us His strategy concerning the situation, we will both win.

Understand that reconciliation can never be realized in the atmosphere of accusation. We must be willing to put away the words that blame and shame; speaking words that uplift and encourage will bring peace and resolution into our situation and relationship. We must allow the Holy Spirit to guide us in every area of our lives.

Principle 2—Open Ears, Shut Mouth

Most of the time, we want to be heard, but we are not as eager to listen. Hearing is key to bringing a proper response and preventing anger from rising. Healthy communication begins with a listening ear. When you only seek to be heard, you diminish the value of the other person's voice and opinion in the relationship.

To keep anger from entering and governing your conversation, always seek to hear the heart of your spouse. If you listen, you will refrain from speaking. We should listen carefully to our spouse and ponder what they say. Refrain from reacting when you hear something that rubs you the wrong way. Doing this will help prevent you from becoming angry and upset.

> Remember this, my dear brothers and sisters: Everyone should be quick to listen, slow to speak, and not get angry easily (James 1:19, GW).

My mother always told me that I was born talking. She and my father were torn between naming me Stacey or Wendy. As I got older, they questioned their choice of names due to my lack of discipline to control my tongue. The love of talking has not always been my greatest asset and has caused me as much grief as it has pleasure. Many people say I have never met a stranger and can stir up conversation with anyone, but my need to speak and be heard has sometimes led to hurtful things coming out of my mouth, things which bore no good fruit.

You Have Two Ears and One Mouth

There is a reason God gave us two ears and just one mouth. If we learn to listen and heed others, rather than always being the one who needs to be heard and understood, then we can have an actual conversation. So often, we refer to a monologue as a dialogue when we are the only ones speaking. We are not carrying on a conversation if we dominate the situation with our own thoughts and opinions, giving no place for others to be heard. At that time, it becomes nothing more than a lecture.

It is imperative to respect one another and allow both parties to express their thoughts and opinions, even if opposing. We need to consider the feelings and thoughts of our spouse. If we never allow them to express themselves, we will communicate that we are not interested in what they have to say, thus making them feel as if their opinions or feelings don't matter. If we are always talking and never listening, we will cause the other person to shut down and feel disinterested in engaging in conversations. If your spouse is never given a place to express their heart fully, they will eventually cease attempting to share it with you.

Breakthrough Comes to Listeners

Being in the ministry for over forty years has afforded us the opportunity to counsel many couples. We have dealt with all kinds of marital situations, from simple things that were easily solved to situations that seemed insurmountable. Without fail, the ones in which we saw breakthroughs, restoration, and resolution were the ones where both parties listened and applied instruction and counsel. Finding a resolution to situations is impossible if you are unwilling to listen. Again, listening is arguably the most critical part of fruitful conversation and communication.

Pride within someone's heart will say, "*I know it all and have all the answers.*" However, humility enables us to close our mouths and open our ears. Remember this: If you want to be heard, you must sow seeds of listening. It is amazing what can happen in your relationship when you begin to hear and value what your spouse has to say. This requires you to truly listen without processing your response before they even finish speaking. Refuse to hear things from a defensive posture. Desire to understand their thoughts and feelings on the issues.

Remember, James said to be quick to listen and slow to speak (James 1:19). Most marital arguments could be avoided if we put this simple principle into practice. Strife will cease when both spouses feel they are heard and valued. I encourage you to try it and see what occurs in your conversation and relationship.

Principle 3—Be Kind

> A gentle answer makes anger disappear, but a rough answer makes it grow (Proverbs 15:1, ERV).

Have you ever heard the statement, "Kill them with kindness"? This saying literally means to respond to aggression and animosity with kindness to diffuse tension. It is a way in which we show that love conquers all. A combative answer will not make anger disappear. If you want the constant cycle of anger and arguments to cease, begin to act upon this rule. Watch what you say, how you say it, and always be kind. Always consider your tone, inflections, and body language. A smile will always endear someone to you, whereas a disgusting scowl will only alienate them.

Have you ever spoken to someone who has nothing good to say about anybody or anything? If so, you are aware that they are some of the most challenging people to be around and just as difficult to love. It requires extra grace and patience to do so. Maybe you are married to someone like that, or perhaps you are that person. If so, you are likely to be angry or upset constantly.

If we get into a pattern of constantly finding fault in others, particularly our spouse, it will cause us to be bitter and agitated. The tendency will be to take personal offense for everything said and done. Nothing that anyone does will ever seem to be right. Your perception will be that everyone means to harm you. In response, we will lash out at those we love and regret it after the action. This is no way for anyone to live.

If this is similar to your behavior, let me encourage you to change your perspective. Allow the Holy Spirit to show you how to hear and respond differently. The Bible declares that if we ask anything according to His will, He is faithful to listen and grant our petitions. So, understand this: You are not a lost cause—no one is. We all need the Holy Spirit to enable us to do better.

Say It with A Smile

Often, we are much kinder and more gracious to strangers than we are to those we love most. We become comfortable with our closest loved ones and know that they love us no matter what! Although this may be true, this attitude and behavior can take a toll on your relationship over time. We must understand that without change and repentance, irreconcilable damage can be done.

The Bible says, "A merry heart does good, like medicine, but a broken spirit dries the bones" (Proverbs 17:22). When you speak to others, especially your spouse, say it with a smile. Choose to believe the best in others and see the good in them. These actions cause your conversation to be different. You will no longer see everything as a personal attack and will be able to respond in a kind and gentle manner. You will endear people to you rather than drive them away.

Contemplate what you are going to say. Then, think about the best way to say it. You must also realize that thinking or feeling something at a given moment does not necessitate it being stated. If it cannot be said in a gentle and kind way, it will most likely stir up something undesirable. Use your words wisely because a gentle answer, as opposed to a sarcastic or rude comment, will remove anger from your heart, as well as others.

Principle 4—Avoid Antagonistic Cliches

Robert and I had to learn early in our relationship to refrain from making antagonistic statements. Many couples keep each other bound to past actions using statements like "you never" or "you always." These things are typically said to control the situation or circumstance. Unfortunately, this is usually a verbal attack on the very person you should love the most. It is accusatory in nature and produces adverse effects within the marriage relationship. Statements like this do not bring resolution; they produce defensiveness and strife. This is a road that leads to nowhere.

Statements that bring accusations, stir up strife, and foster division are unhealthy. The Bible says it is pleasant when we dwell in unity with one another. It also says that God commands His blessing where people are united. I would rather live under the blessing than the curse. Refraining from accusatory statements will keep strife and division away. However, lending your tongue to criticize and blame your spouse will surely open "a can of worms" that will become hard to contain.

When you go down this road of criticism, one thing leads to another, and before you know what happened, you are cursing the very person you vowed to love, honor, protect, and cherish for a lifetime. Before you know it, you are archenemies instead of lovers and partners. You find yourself caught up in word wars where no one wins. Your words and accusations have only produced hurt and pain that now have to heal.

It is essential to put away words that remind our spouse of their past sins or the hurt they caused. Rehearsing these things only declares that you have not truly forgiven and moved on. For the sake of the longevity of our marriages, we cannot live in the past. We must not hold our partner captive to their past actions by these constant reminders. It is not healthy for our marriage or our own personal lives. We must speak words of life and blessing to each other.

Let It Begin with Me

Imagine a marriage without strife, condemnation, and shame. Envision how it would be without walking daily through a verbal minefield. Think about a marriage where you always speak words that build up and bless—a marriage where you enjoy each other and the life you are building together. You may have laughed aloud, thinking, "*This could never happen to me.*" However, it can! Change your perspective and say, "*Lord, let it start with me.*"

We must take captive our own words and thoughts if we want to see a breakthrough in our marriage. If your attitude says, "*You don't know who I'm married to,*" you are merely blaming your spouse. Your belief about your spouse will cause your marriage to remain stagnant. We are not responsible for our spouse's actions or words, but we are accountable for our own and can choose to believe the best about them. Taking responsibility for your words, actions, and beliefs is where godly relationships begin. Pray that God will let it begin with you!

Putting God at the center of your marriage starts with you. It starts with you putting a watch over your mouth and choosing to believe and speak the best, even in the tough times. I have said it often: seed sown is harvest reaped. What do you want to reap in your marriage? Sow the seeds for the harvest you desire.

Principle 5—Ask Questions Rather than Accuse

As discussed in principle #4, no good fruit comes from accusations! So, rather than accusing, we must replace the allegation with a question. There are several ways this can be done.

A question can be accusatory in nature. So, you must be careful in the way you pose your question. For instance, you can say, "*Why are you angry?*" Or you can say, "*Are you upset?*" Do you see the difference? One example has already determined that your spouse is angry and upset, while the other brings no judgment and gives them the opportunity to explain their disposition.

Resolution cannot be found in the atmosphere of accusation. It is important that we do not place ourselves in the position of judge and jury with our spouse. We must have grace and give them the benefit of the doubt. Often, we think that since we "know" our spouse, we understand precisely how and why they are acting or responding in a certain way. We come to conclusions concerning their attitude because of our familiarity with them. However, this is not the correct thing to do because we can be wrong.

Don't Judge, Rather Encourage

The truth is that we all have bad days and have been overcome by the stresses of life. So, if your spouse acts differently, that does not necessarily equate to being upset or angry. Refrain from becoming their judge by accusing your spouse's attitude. Sometimes, people need to process the things they are going through. It does not mean it is your fault or that they are upset with you.

I put myself in that position on many occasions in the past. If something was off, I believed it was my fault. This disposition will go nowhere that is good. It leads down the road of frustration for your spouse when being forced to explain their actions. Sometimes, we merely need to be there to encourage and uplift our spouse. We do not always need to know everything; instead, we should be the voice of encouragement and peace in what may be a challenging time for them.

Again, "It's not what you say, but how you say it." That is such a true principle. You must ask the Lord to put a watch over your mouth and think before you speak. Take thought not to lace your questions with accusations. Refuse to allow your moment of frustration to be expressed verbally with words that hurt. Examine your conversation habits and adjust them. If you do, I know you will see things change in your life and marriage.

Ask Yourself

When you speak to your spouse, are your words sweet as honey or like fingernails on a chalkboard? Do you desire to listen to your spouse, or do you just want to be heard? Are you quick to accuse your partner and defend yourself? Is it more important for you to be declared right than to be reconciled with your mate? Many conflicts can be avoided if we choose the proper perspective and approach. Through a ***sheer commitment***, you can make the right choice every time.

13

Tend to Your Garden

Do you remember when you were dating and had no care in the world? All you wanted to do was be together and enjoy each other's company. When you were apart, you could not wait to see each other; when you were together, you never wanted it to end. You were in love, and you relished your time together. These are wonderful times that often become just a memory.

We have seen this dynamic happen repeatedly. Two people get married and then let the cares and stresses of life come in and choke out the making of any future memories. We must learn to relax, enjoy each other, and put away the cares of this life that screams for attention. It is important to take a little time to smell the roses. Your spouse will thank you, and it will make your relationship stronger.

The pressures of life try to keep us from the things that are most important. Your marriage and your spouse are primary. Making time to have fun and enjoy one another's company will pay off in dividends that will go beyond any extra dollar or deal you can make on your job. It will pay off in points greater than any of your sports teams have ever scored. It is vital to STOP… then enjoy life together.

You Married Your Best Friend

At one time, you and your spouse were best friends. Sadly, many forget that friendship after getting married and only focus on the daily grind and occasional sex. It takes more than a clean house, three square meals a day, a paycheck, and a sex life to have a great marriage.

You did not get married to have a maid or a sugar daddy! You also did not marry your spouse just for passionate sex, which is a wonderful experience you share with your life-partner. However, you married your best friend! You married the person who could make you laugh when you were sad or cry simply because of the sweet and thoughtful actions and sacrifices they made to be with you. We must remember and reenact the friendship with our spouse and all the fun we had before marrying—the thrill we experienced by just being together and enjoying each other's company.

Men and women alike desire to be loved and appreciated. There is nothing that shouts love like giving your time and attention. Flowers fade, chocolates turn into fat cells, and though diamonds may last forever, they pale in comparison to time truly spent together with no distractions.

The Value of Time Together

There is nothing more significant than time spent with just your spouse. It can be a walk on the beach, a ride in the car, a mall trip to window shop, a fishing trip in the early morning hours, or just staying home watching a movie while eating popcorn together. Regardless of the activity, it is imperative to take time together.

At the end of your life, a wife will not wish for another bouquet of flowers, and a husband won't covet another favorite home-cooked meal. On the contrary, you will wish you just had one more moment together. You will long for one more opportunity to spend time together holding hands and having one more conversation about the memories you share. There is no greater time to start than now. No one is stopping you. Do it today!

There is nothing more miserable than a life consisting of going through the daily grind with no relational enjoyment because it only leads to discontentment and discouragement. Unfortunately, if this is not addressed, it will cause a wedge to be driven between you and your spouse.

Keep On Dating

I recall a couple that Robert and I counseled years ago. Due to their busy life and work schedules, she began to feel unappreciated and devalued. They owned a business and were together every day. However, they still felt like they never spent any time with one another. Their business had consumed them, and they needed boundaries for both work and family. Some of the best advice they were given was to begin to date again. Yes, you should date your spouse.

Where is it written that you can no longer date your spouse once you are married? You need time to unplug from the daily minutia. Get off the hamster wheel and focus on each other's needs and desires. I have seen marriages end in divorce because they simply lost interest in their respective spouses. Why did this happen? It was because they failed at making time to foster continued interest in each other. They stopped doing the things that sparked their relationship in the beginning.

This behavior leads to what is called irreconcilable differences in divorce courts. However, more often, it is a loss of interest that produces a canyon of separation between them. If they continued dating like they did when they first met, their marriage would have succeeded.

Always Pursue Your Spouse

Before they married, their future spouse was the object of their attention. They pursued one another and did special things to woo the love of their life. However, the pursuit ended once they were captured, and the ring went on the finger. The truth is you should always be in pursuit of your spouse. You should never lose the "chase" for their heart. If you do, someone else will come along and show them the attention you fail to give. It is worth the effort. You thought they were worth it before the "I do's" were said, and they still are today. Think about it!

When counseling couples who have fallen into this trap of "we don't have anything in common" or "I just don't have feelings for him/her anymore," we often assign them a simple yet much-needed exercise. We ask them to write down ten things that attracted them to each other. It is amazing how love can be stirred up if we allow ourselves to go down memory lane and simply remember the little things.

Memory Lane

When Robert and I were dating, if I was sad, he would do this thing: close his eyes tight, look at me, and say these words,

"Look into my eyes." I know it is corny and sounds silly. If you know my husband, it is so out of character for him, yet he did it to cheer me up. Without fail, every time, it made me laugh. Then he would kiss me, and all my sadness would be gone—all because of one silly gesture that was out of character for him. However, he was willing to look like a fool for love. What did your spouse do to make you laugh or feel loved? What did you do to make your spouse feel appreciated and needed? Perhaps you should both do it again!

Let me encourage you to take a trip down memory lane. Recall what attracted you to your spouse. What made you laugh and want to be together forever? When you feel like all hope is gone and your feelings of love have flown out the window, take a scenic journey through the portals of the memories. Think about the wonderful times that you shared with one another. It's worth the trip, and you will be glad you did!

> Abstain from all appearance of evil. And the very God of peace sanctify you wholly; and I pray God your whole spirit and soul and body be preserved blameless unto the coming of our Lord Jesus Christ (1 Thessalonians 5:22-23, KJV).

Regardless of your situation, you should NEVER allow anyone to be closer to you than your spouse. This behavior is asking for trouble. No work partner or friend, whether male or female, should ever be allowed to enter that space—absolutely no one. Allowing anyone to invade this territory is certainly a recipe for disaster and possibly divorce. If someone is closer to you than your spouse, they are too close. You should never share your most intimate thoughts and desires with anyone except your spouse. You should never be in a place that gives the appearance of evil.

Repeatedly, I have observed couples who fail to cultivate a life together while blaming their spouse for the disconnectedness in their marital relationship. Each spouse accepted no responsibility for ignoring their marriage. They failed to fulfill their partner's needs and desires while complaining about their own desires going unmet. I want to encourage you to take time and make an investment in your marriage. The time you invest will cost you nothing compared to the dividends it will pay. Take time to smell the roses and live a life that will bring joy and fulfillment to you and your spouse.

The Big Lie—Divorce

Divorce is so easy and completely acceptable today. For a few hundred dollars and a signature, you can be a free bird. Unfortunately, the statistics in the church are not much better than those in the world. We have come to terms with the notion that if we do not like our spouse anymore, we can just divorce. If they no longer make us giggle and give us butterflies in our bellies, we just divorce them. If our spouse no longer lives up to the perfect television wife or husband, or they no longer sexually satisfy us, that is reason enough to move on to greener pastures.

Unfortunately, in the minds of many, divorce has become the road to freedom and happiness. Today's society has made it easy to justify our choice to move on when we are no longer satisfied. Everything is centered around how we feel at a given moment since we are constantly told that our feelings are the most important thing. We deserve to be happy. After all, we only get one life; we should live it to the fullest. Unfortunately, this line of thinking fails to consider the collateral damage that takes place.

I understand that there are legitimate reasons for divorce, and in no way am I desiring to shame anyone. However, if you are remarried or plan to remarry, I trust this book will help you remain with your present spouse. It is my desire to help you have the God-kind of marriage that will last until your final breath together.

Your Spouse Is Not a Car

Too many people today trade spouses like they trade cars. Once the new smell wears off or they start to have a little rattle, they head to the car lot and shop for a newer model. This trend in marriages is unfortunate and should not be happening. People are not disposable, and neither is your marriage. There are many more reasons to stay with your spouse than to separate from them.

You can have a marriage made in heaven if you simply invite the Holy Spirit to do a work in you and your spouse. We have watched seemingly impossible and unredeemable relationships be transformed supernaturally. It is amazing what will happen if you focus on fixing the person in the mirror. Then, you can have your eyes fixed on each other and, together, fix your eyes on the "Fixer," the Holy Spirit. He will do great things within your marriage if you only allow Him that place in your life.

Give Attention to Your Lawn

Again, many have said that "the grass is greener on the other side." Some say this because they are disenchanted with where they are and what they have. However, if you consider for a minute what makes the grass greener, you may think twice before wanting to visit or pitch your tent in that pasture.

Manure is used to make grass greener, which means fecal matter makes it look good. Many times, what looks enticing from a distance has a stench and smell that is undesirable. Today, some people are trading in their precious property for a place that only looks beautiful from afar. However, it is littered with things that stink, and you have to tip-toe through it to avoid being covered with the stench. Think about it!

Let's look at it from a different perspective. My husband and I use a lawn service for our home. During the winter season, our grass goes dormant. However, this does not mean it can't be beautiful and green again. On the contrary, our lawn service will fertilize our grass at the beginning of the spring season. Slowly, as the weather begins to warm and the spring rain falls, our grass turns green again. Before you know it, our yard is beautiful and has no trace of the dormancy it once had.

At the moment, your marriage may look dark and possibly seem dead. Think about this: Perhaps it is only dormant and needs some attention. Maybe it just needs some time, some watering, and some warmth. It may not be as pretty as your neighbor's, but with a little attention and a little time, your marriage can be beautiful and lush again. The grass is not always greener; it just needs your attention.

Be Willing to Work

Many today want a great marriage and family but do not want to put in the work to make it happen. They are too busy making a buck, hanging with friends, and having their "me time." There is much talk today about "self-care." I understand the need to take care of yourself, but you must remember that life is not all about you.

We can get so caught up in our needs and desires that we ignore the care of our spouse. Are you caring for your spouse, or is it just all about you? Are you tending to the needs and desires of your partner or just expecting them to be happy and fulfilled by your presence? Remember, having a beautiful lawn takes work. It takes some tender loving care. Likewise, a beautiful marriage requires diligence and work.

You Might Get Dirty

Truthfully, growing plants has never been my specialty. I love a lush, beautiful yard and garden, but I fail to make it happen. Every year, as spring approaches, I dream about it, look at pictures on social media sites, and desire to have my house look just like the ones on the cover of the most popular magazines.

In the past, I have walked through the garden center at my favorite stores, purchased a few plants, and attempted to give it a go, only to fail. I forget how much work, time, and money go into having my dream garden. Unfortunately, the thought of the amount of labor required to have this consistently hinders me from doing it. The truth is I do not like getting dirty and working in the garden.

In the same way, many dream of the perfect marriage, like the ones on social media or in bridal magazines. However, they don't see the work, time, selfless acts, and sacrifice required to achieve it. In successful marriages, there are times when things get messy and dirty, but spouses choose to love, forgive, and move forward. They continue to love even when the thorns are poking them. They water, fertilize, and pay attention to their spouse, not just their own personal desires.

Seasons Change

Your marriage will not always look like a beautiful garden. You will go through seasons. Most plants do not blossom all year, but that does not mean they will never bloom again. You must choose to be faithful in continuing to do your part to cause your marital relationship to grow until the flowers bloom again. Remember, it may be dormant, but it is not dead.

You may feel as though your life and marriage are in a season of dormancy, and if so, you must be careful not to regret the decision you made in choosing your spouse. The feeling of "I picked the wrong person" or "I picked a dud" is toxic to a marriage. You did not choose the wrong person; they just need some attention and time. Do not simply throw away your prize rose because it has yet to bloom. The season you are in will change, and it will be beautiful once again.

It is essential to keep your eye single—don't let your eyes wander into comparing your marriage to someone else's. It is unwise to compare yourself to others because you do not know the struggles they experience. Doing this will always lead down the road to "if only" or "I should have," which opens doors for the enemy to fuel doubt and instability. The Bible says that a double-minded man is unstable in all his ways. It also warns of the dangers of comparison with others.

> Of course, we wouldn't dare to put ourselves in the same class or compare ourselves with those who rate themselves so highly. They compare

> themselves to one another and make up their own standards to measure themselves by, and then they judge themselves by their own standards. What self-delusion! (2 Corinthians 10:12, TPT).

I know of some who have allowed their hearts to question their choice and then connect with old friends from their past lives via social media. In no time, they were meeting, reminiscing, and reliving the past. Later, it became an adulterous affair. It only takes one moment, one choice, and one click on the keyboard to go off the rails. That is why it is so important to keep your eye single.

My husband asks, "Why would I want hamburger when I already have a filet mignon?" Of course, he doesn't view me as a piece of meat, but rather his premium choice. Really, who wants potted meat when they already have steak? Yet, if we begin to look elsewhere and allow our hearts to become contaminated, we will bring a breach into our marriage and home. Do not let your heart go down the road of regret.

Instead of reconnecting with an old friend from your past, connect with your spouse. Reminisce with the love of your life and allow feelings to be reignited. Do not spend your time attempting to rekindle a dead relationship from the past; instead, invest your time and energy into making your marriage better than it has ever been.

Hollywood Fantasy

Hollywood can paint an unrealistic picture of what love and relationships should look like. Remember, it is all staged, scripted, and scheduled. It takes an army of people for them to portray their perfect picture of love, yet it is only pretend and make-believe. However, putting Jesus at the center of your love story will make a wonderful film called "Your Best Life Together."

We cannot allow a counterfeit to trick us into longing for something that is not real. God has planned a better marriage for you. The real thing that you can experience with your spouse is better. At the end of the day, my spouse is not an actor who leaves the set; he meets me in bed. He rubs my back at night and wakes up beside me in the morning. He is my best friend and lover every day and in every season. He is better than anything that Hollywood can portray.

It is amazing what can happen if you begin to reminisce with your spouse about what you have experienced together. Everything Robert and I have gone through has not been wonderful; we have faced many challenges. Amazing breakthroughs in our lives have made us cry with joy. We have also made difficult decisions where it was hard to reach a place of agreement, but we made it through. We have experienced some overwhelmingly great times together and some really tough times. There have been highs, and we have had lows. However, we have weathered the storms, and they have made us stronger together.

Today, I am so thankful for every life experience we have shared. Those things now give us memories for a lifetime—memories I want to share with no one other than him. Robert is the one I chose; he is God's best for me. I am thankful I made the right choice, and so did you!

Ask Yourself

What are you doing regularly to make your relationship better? Do you set aside dedicated time with your spouse to enjoy time together? Are there moments when you recall the good times you experienced with one another? How much value do you place on your marriage, and what will you contribute to improving it? The truth is you will only get out of something what you put into it. ***Sheer commitment*** to sow the seeds of time and attention in your marriage will yield a great harvest of blessings!

14

Fire in the Furnace

Let's get real as we talk about what the Bible has to say about sex! It seems that this is a topic avoided by many pastors. Rarely are things taught or discussed concerning this important topic that the Bible articulates clearly for us. It appears to be one of those things that we don't want to talk about. However, we are going to discuss biblical principles regarding this issue.

Many today think sex is not only a dirty word but also a taboo subject that should just be worked out between husband and wife with little to no guidance. I am unsure why sexual relationships are something that the church at large refuses to mention or teach from the pulpits. The Bible talks about it in a very exact and candid way.

Sex Needs to Be Taught in the Church

Early within our pastoral ministry, my husband and I learned that the subject of sex within the marriage covenant was something we should not only focus on in private counseling sessions but realized it was something that should be taught in the pulpit. Robert often says, "There may be snow on the rooftop, but there is still fire in the furnace." We are always affectionate and not ashamed to express our love and desire for one another appropriately. This behavior is the way God created us to respond to each other.

Is it possible that if the church taught biblical truths concerning the subject of sex, married couples might not have the struggles surrounding this vital aspect of their relationship? If we taught young people that sex is both commanded and blessed by the Lord in the sacred union of marriage, would more people save their virginity until married? Think about it.

If the church shares the truth in a bold and accurate way, couples will experience freedom and fulfillment in their marriages. Sexual issues will be minimized as biblical understanding blossoms. Perhaps the reason humanistic secular sex education has risen in our schools, along with its controversy, is due to our failure to address the subject properly within the church.

Marriage is more than a legal contract; it is a heart covenant. You did not get married just to keep each other company or have a two-income household to pay bills. Couples marry for communion with their spouse. You exchange vows with one another to fulfill the very desires placed in you by the heavenly Father. It is not abnormal or strange to desire sexual fulfillment. However, God purposed this to happen only within the marriage covenant.

> Then the Lord God took the man and put him in the garden of Eden to tend and keep it. And the Lord God commanded the man, saying, "Of every tree of the garden you may freely eat; but of the tree of the knowledge of good and evil you shall not eat, for in the day that you eat

> of it you shall surely die." And the Lord God said, "It is not good that man should be alone; I will make him a helper comparable to him." ...And the Lord God caused a deep sleep to fall on Adam, and he slept; and He took one of his ribs, and closed up the flesh in its place. Then the rib which the Lord God had taken from man He made into a woman, and brought her to the man. And Adam said: "This is now bone of my bones and flesh of my flesh; She shall be called Woman, because she was taken out of Man." Therefore, a man shall leave his father and mother and be joined to his wife, and they shall become one flesh. And they were both naked, the man and his wife, and were not ashamed (Genesis 2:15-18, 21-25).

On the sixth day of creation, God created man. Then, He said it was not good for man to be alone. So, He created woman to be a helper for him. Adam was put into a deep sleep, and a rib was taken from his side. It was from this rib that God formed and created woman. After He had made her, God presented the woman to Adam in all her glory. Adam said, "This is now bone of my bone and flesh of my flesh; She shall be called Woman..." (Genesis 2:23). Adam liked what he saw and was physically attracted to her. To Adam, she was incomparable to all God had previously created. Eve was God's crowning creation. She was as they say, "Just what the doctor ordered."

God Did It Right!

Before we dig deeper into the subject of sex in marriage, let me make one thing clear: God did it right in the beginning when he created one man and one woman. This is the only union that the Lord recognizes. After He created man and woman, He stepped back and called it "good."

You fit with your spouse like a puzzle piece because you were created for one another. It does not matter how many laws are passed or what any worldly judge says; God said the marriage covenant was between one man and one woman. He gave no other combination than this! If God said it, then that settles it.

Homosexuality is not the plan of God. Polyamory, having multiple partners, is not the plan of God. Having an "open" marriage is not in His plan. Man with animals is not God's design. If it were, there would have been no reason to create Eve. None of these sexual perversions endorsed in our culture will ever be acceptable in the eyes of God. They are and will always be sinful and lead to bondage and death. Again, God's command is for one man and one woman in covenant to experience a sexual relationship with only each other.

When we were children, our picture Bibles illustrated Adam with a loincloth, Eve with a ripped cloth skirt, and her hair covering her breast. However, there was no cover until after they sinned. Before the fall, they were naked! They lived in the Garden of Eden without a stitch of clothing. The Scripture declares that they were naked and not ashamed. Truthfully, if my husband and I are in a room together and naked, there are definitely going to be some fireworks that happen. He desires me, and I desire him. God made us that way. In case you are unsure, He made you that way also. You should not feel shameful about sex within the context of the marriage covenant.

Safety in the Marriage Bed

We have witnessed couples who struggle because of shame and insecurity. These issues can originate due to physical appearance, past sin, or past trauma such as rape or molestation. Many people wrestle with these things on varying levels. However, just as Jesus can heal all matters of sickness and disease, He can heal your self-image, heart, and emotions. God created you to find pleasure in sex with your spouse.

Understand that the marriage bed is a safe place. Your spouse loves you because you are his/her gift from God. They love you and desire to be with you and be sexually intimate with you. This attitude is not dirty or inordinate because God designed it. There is safety when you are in the arms of one another.

> Nevertheless, because of sexual immorality, let each man have his own wife, and let each woman have her own husband. Let the husband render to his wife the affection due her, and likewise also the wife to her husband [sexually satisfy one another]. The wife does not have authority over her own body, but the husband does. And likewise, the husband does not have authority over his own body, but the wife does. Do not deprive one another except with consent for a time, that you may give yourselves to fasting and prayer; and come together again so that Satan does not tempt you because of your lack of self-control [you cannot rightfully deprive one another] (1 Corinthians 7:2-5, emphasis added).

After God created the woman and presented her to Adam, He commanded them to be fruitful and multiply. He told them to have babies. Multiplication cannot happen absent a sexual relationship.

If sex were wrong, God would have created a different means by which the world could be populated. However, He did not, and we get pleasure from the act of procreation. At the same time, sexual intimacy should not cease once you are no longer desirous to have children or are past a certain age. We were created to pleasure one another for a lifetime.

Unity and Oneness

We are commanded to give ourselves to our spouse and not withhold affection. Sex should never be focused on your personal gratification; it should always be mutually satisfying. The aim should be for you to bring pleasure to your spouse. The physical and emotional connection that the act of intimacy brings is amazing. It releases endorphins in your body that are only released during sexual intercourse. This is the way that God created it to be.

Biophysics has revealed that when a husband and wife are together in a sexual act, a chemical reaction happens in the human brain (vasopressin and oxytocin) that has the same effect as an addictive drug euphoria. This means that a man and woman become connected on a deep, addictive level during their sexual encounters. It could be said that every man should be addicted to his wife, and every wife should be addicted to her husband because sex develops a reliance and a oneness with your spouse.

Sharing your body with your spouse brings comfort and safety. You will find that emotional security, transparency, and communication will increase when you are sexually active with your spouse. God initiated this closeness when He commanded man to be fruitful and multiply.

Years ago, my husband and I were talking to some minister friends. During our conversation, they said, "Making love to your spouse runs the devil off." Sex with your spouse brings a closeness the enemy cannot penetrate. This unity is one of the most powerful tools that married couples have to stop the devil from attacking our marriages. Together, as you express your needs, desires, and emotions, you can have intimacy and closeness even in what seems to be the most difficult situations.

The Deepest Expression

It is essential to express your deep feelings for your spouse. It is equally vital to tell them they are beautiful/handsome. Everyone wants to be celebrated and feel special. You should believe your spouse is the best thing since "sliced bread" and God's perfect match for you. It is amazing what speaking words of validation to your spouse will do for your sex life.

My husband constantly says things to validate and celebrate me. Anyone who has heard him minister or been with us knows this is true. He is not silent about his feelings for me and makes me feel loved and desired. He constantly calls me his "brick house," even though I do not meet the qualifications per the song. If you desire a better sex life, you may want to check your words to one another.

The sexual relationship does not begin naked in the bedroom; it starts in the living room with words of love and endearment. While men are usually like microwaves and ready for sex at any moment, women are not. Wives usually need time accompanied by words and actions of love and affirmation. The things that spouses speak to one another will determine the level of connectedness that happens during the act of sex.

I/You Have Issues

I am aware that some may have certain medical, physical, or psychological conditions that cause the need to approach sexual intercourse differently or may even prohibit participation in a conventional manner. This chapter is not to condemn or bring shame but to bring light to the issues that married couples need to shore up in the area of intimacy within their relationship.

Perhaps you struggle due to psychological conditions because of trauma you experienced before or even while married. The enemy would like nothing more than to hold you captive to a negative traumatic experience. In these cases, it is essential that open and honest communication takes place between husband and wife. There needs to be an understanding of possible triggers or things that may cause reliving that hurt or trauma. I believe healing and deliverance can take place, and you can live in a state of total and complete freedom from your history. In these situations, both husband and wife must approach intimacy with grace and understanding. During the healing process, both spouses should do everything in their power to ensure their partner's physical and emotional needs are met. It is vital to a healthy marriage for both husband and wife to be honest and transparent.

If you face physical difficulty in your sexual relationship, you may need to seek medical advice from your doctor or try a holistic avenue to solve certain sexual dysfunctions. Seek medical advice when needed, but I encourage you not to ignore the situation. Do what is necessary to receive the help you need. It is vital to your relationship to maintain a healthy sex life.

As we age, menopause can wreak havoc on a woman, both emotionally and often physically. I encourage you to be open with your husband and speak with your doctor. You may find simple yet effective things that will help you continue to find pleasure in your sexual experience. Too many times, we (speaking from experience) begin to have changes in our bodies that may cause fear. This kind of fear causes us to withdraw rather than be open and honest about our experiences and feelings. Know this: fear is straight from the pit and should never hold you back or separate you from experiencing intimacy with your spouse. Many men may also experience changes as they age. However, all of this can be overcome, and intimacy between a husband and wife can continue to thrive with simple conversation, understanding, and honesty.

Maybe you are a couple who struggle due to medical or physical situations. First of all, do not be ashamed to talk to your spouse to find a solution, ensuring that both of you are being satisfied physically, emotionally, and sexually. Each spouse should be compassionate and understanding when physical issues need to be overcome.

Keep Your Bed Undefiled

Sadly, many have mistakenly understood that marriage is a license to participate in ungodly behavior in the bedroom, thus defiling sexual acts with their spouse. However, the writer of Hebrews exhorts us to keep the marriage bed undefiled. Scripture actually places responsibility on the husband and wife to KEEP the bed undefiled. This admonition means they do not need anything other than each other to bring satisfaction and gratification to one another.

> Marriage must be honored among all and the marriage bed kept undefiled, for God will judge sexually immoral people and adulterers (Hebrews 13:4, NET).

We are commanded to keep the bed undefiled. No marriage should have a disposition of "anything goes" in the bedroom. It is shocking and overwhelming the number of Christians who think pornographic objects (sex toys) or videos are acceptable within the confines of the marriage. Some people think if another person is not physically involved, then anything goes. My friend, this is simply not the truth. When God made you and your spouse, He created you with everything you needed to bring pleasure to each other. No pornographic item or video is needed!

These things that have become acceptable in the bedroom need to be exposed for what they are. A fake penis is equivalent to having sex with another man. Inserting manufactured things inside the vagina for the purpose of sexual arousal or fulfillment is a perversion. The same goes for men and some of the things that are created today to achieve arousal and climax. These things should not be brought into the bedroom of any marriage.

Addiction to Perversion

Pornography today is a seventeen-billion-dollar industry in the United States and is readily available to everyone at the click of a button. It is sad to think that some Christians introduce this into their marriage. I do not want my husband to be aroused by another woman on a screen while making love to me. This behavior is perverted and wrong. I am there to arouse him, and he needs nothing else. Likewise, I do not need or want anything but him to bring pleasure to me. I do not need to watch other people commit fornication on a television screen to be aroused sexually.

Unfortunately, pornography is an addiction to which many have fallen prey. It is deceptive, and some believers see nothing sinful or wrong with watching it. All the while, it is destroying their marriage. Pornography has resulted in the demise of intimacy in exchange for lust and animalistic desire. Sexual intercourse becomes merely a physical exchange or transaction between two people in a bed that is absent of emotional connection. Why is this? It is because their sex life is based on the stimulation they receive from looking at someone other than the person they married.

Several studies have found a link between compulsive pornography use and reduced sex drive for a physical person, namely, your spouse. Sexual relationships that seek intimacy will not turn to pornographic means for fulfillment. God's design for your relationship is to keep the bedroom pure and undefiled. God created you to be fully capable of fulfilling your spouse's needs, and we must seek to fulfill one another and remove all distractions and ungodly actions.

Lack of Prioritization

We must make a time and place for intimacy in our relationship. It is funny that before we are married, the enemy will do everything to get us into bed together. However, once we are married, he will do everything to keep us out of bed together.

When we are first married, sex is all new and exciting. Intimacy is easier because we seem to have fewer responsibilities and less distractions. As life progresses, we get busy—having babies and raising children, which turns into added responsibility and activity. We become taxi drivers, maids, coaches, cooks, teachers, lawyers settling disputes, and the list goes on. As our responsibilities increase, we fail to prioritize our time together. However, this is when we need to make it paramount. Sex with our spouse should never get "old hat" or common, and most of all, dismissed and forgotten. You must make time to be intimate with your spouse.

Thursday at 8:00 pm

We often have marriage and family seminars around Valentine's Day. During our conferences, we usually have time for questions and answers. I remember a question being asked to a couple on the panel concerning how they made time for each other since they kept a busy schedule. I was shocked at their answer. It was just simple and matter-of-fact. They said, "We put it on the calendar every Thursday at 8 o'clock." This couple understood the importance of their time together and the need for intimacy to continue to have a healthy and happy marriage. So, they did whatever it took to make it happen.

I am not saying you must make an appointment with your spouse for sexual intercourse or that you abandon spontaneity. Being spontaneous is a wonderful thing and can keep your marriage and sex life exciting. However, if your lifestyle demands a date on the calendar, be willing to do that. It is better to have scheduled sexual intercourse regularly than infrequent spontaneity with occasional intimacy.

Active and Healthy

Sex should be anticipated and celebrated, not just tolerated. It is a beautiful act designed by the Lord, not the devil. Some people just go through the motions and find no physical joy in the act of sex. However, God designed for each partner to be satisfied and fulfilled.

Married Christian couples should have the most active and healthy sex lives of any group of people on the planet. I have heard my husband say from the pulpit, "Sex should be like church attendance; you should be faithful to be there at least once a week—three times preferably." If you think this is strong, read the Song of Solomon.

You must prioritize your marriage and do what is needed to keep the sparks alive. When we counsel couples, we encourage date nights, time away, and frequency of sex. It is unhealthy for your relationship to be void of dedicated, uninterrupted time with one another. Husbands should take time to make their wives a priority. They will reap the benefits of that thoughtfulness and sacrifice. This is undoubtedly a recipe for a happy wife. Again, you know the saying, "Happy wife, happy life!"

Improper Expectations

Mentioned earlier was the analogy that men are like microwaves and women are like crockpots. This comparison perfectly describes most couples and the roles they play in a sexual relationship together. A man is like a racehorse; lift the gate, and they are off to the races as fast as they can go. They need very little preparation time or coaxing to have sex.

Most women are not that way. They need more time and attention. They desire to know and feel loved. A woman needs time to warm up at the moment and then savor it like a five-star, five-course meal. They do not want a trip to a drive-thru window. It is vital for both husband and wife to realize each other's makeup and desires. Failure to do so will cause both spouses to be frustrated and disappointed in the marriage bed.

It is best for husbands to turn on the crockpot (their wives) when they wake up in the morning and allow things to simmer all day long. A husband's text message to his wife in the middle of a hectic day expressing his love will go a long way. A single rose purchased at the store on your way home from work says you were thinking of her and that she is worth the extra mile. It's amazing how creative you can be in turning up the heat if you just put forth the effort.

Silly Love Songs

My husband is a minister, songwriter, and author. Needless to say, he is very didactic and creative with his words and thoughts. One time, he actually wrote me a really sweet song. However, more than his skillfully written songs, my favorite thing he does is roll over in the mornings and sing me spontaneous silly love songs despite my "shark fin" hair, smeared makeup, pillow-marked face, and morning breath. It immediately endears him to me. He also calls me on the phone when we are apart, and when I answer, he sings, "I just called to say I love you." Things like that begin to spark the flames of love (and he knows that). You do not have to break the bank to do things that will fan the flame of passion.

Just a silly story: In my husband's attempt to be thoughtful, he texted me one day instead of calling me. In the text, he typed, "I just texted to say I love you," and hit send. A response came back immediately, "I love you too!" However, the response was not from me because he had accidentally texted a gentleman from our church and did not realize it until the response returned. He was extremely embarrassed and immediately called to share what happened with me; we both laughed. Now he checks his contact before he hits send. However, it was the thought that counted, and I recognized his intention. Besides, our dear friend and church member got a good laugh out of the entire ordeal.

Be Sensitive to One Another

Women should be sensitive to their husband's needs and desires. You may not always be afforded the slow cooker process you desire, and you may need to be spontaneous to meet his needs. After all, we must remember that sex and fulfillment in the marriage are not merely about us individually. We are meant to give ourselves to our spouse and to tend to their needs. A one-sided, self-centered sex life will only lead to the frustration and possible disengagement of one spouse or the other. It is our responsibility to make sure our spouse is sexually fulfilled.

Likewise, men should understand their wives in the same manner. There are times when she needs to be held and cuddled without any pressure to have intercourse. Sometimes she may be going through challenges that affect her sexual desire. This should not be seen as rejection; rather, it should be understood with care and compassion. Both spouses must exercise sensitivity to one another.

Fulfillment and Intimacy

Couples should have a healthy and active sex life. This happens when you seek to bring fulfillment to your spouse. Seeking only personal fulfillment will leave each spouse with a feeling of emptiness as the result of only going through the motions. Remember, God designed the act of sexual intercourse to connect spouses to one another both physically and emotionally. It should not be merely an act of physical fulfillment for the moment.

We must remember that sex is not dirty or shameful. It was created by God to be enjoyed in the covenant of marriage. If we keep Jesus at the center, we will have bliss in the bedroom. Sexual intimacy will bring unity to you as a couple and will endear you to each other.

If you want to see strife and contention eliminated from your marriage, then maintain a vibrant and active sex life. God commanded that man and woman replenish the earth, which means God blessed sexual intercourse within marriage. We should obey this command just like others in His Word.

Ask Yourself

Think about these questions: Do you value sexual intimacy with your spouse, and is it an essential part of your relationship? Are there things that happened in your life that caused an unfavorable view of sexual intercourse, and is there a need for healing? Do you regularly satisfy your spouse sexually, and do you find closeness when you do? These are not only questions you should ask yourself but also your spouse. Be open and transparent with one another. Make a ***sheer commitment*** to embrace a healthy and fulfilling sexual relationship with your spouse. You will be glad you did, and it will put a smile on your face!

CONCLUSION:
Together We Can Do It!

I want to encourage you that no matter what stage of life you are in, whether it be dreaming about your future spouse, in the process of planning your "big day," newly married, or if you have been married for decades, it is vital to keep Jesus at the center of it all. You must remember that in a marriage relationship, three are better than two. Yes, you heard correctly!

We are destined to succeed when we allow the Lord into our marriage and put away our selfish desires. When we begin to enact principles from the Word of God and allow our own desires and dreams to align with His plans and purposes, His promises become an open door for us to find and obtain peace and joy.

Commitment

Robert and I discovered early in our relationship that commitment was the key to having a successful marriage. Fairy tale dreams are nice, but not reality. No marriage can survive and thrive without the simple principle of commitment. Dreams can become reality, but only with the work that it takes to make them real. Commitment is the starting point for this to happen.

Remember this: It is not about finding the right person but rather being the right person. If we constantly focus on our spouse's shortcomings, we will always fall short of being the godly spouse we were created to be. We need to replace fault-finding with internal soul-searching and allow the Holy Spirit to illuminate things that we ourselves need to change to be that right person. Joy and contentment will not be found in throwing stones but in giving honor and grace to your spouse.

Life is full of challenges, and everything is not always going to be bubbles and butterflies. However, if you choose to make a commitment to always believe the best, see the best, and give your best, you can have joy in the middle of life's trials and challenges that arise.

Divided We Fall

No team wins when they are divided. You must view your spouse as your number one teammate and always work together for the good of the team. Your marriage will never win if you constantly point fingers at each other. This kind of behavior will only lead to one or possibly both parties wanting to throw in the towel and give up.

What if we change our strategy rather than pointing the finger and finding fault? It always takes a change in strategy and mindset to come from behind and win. If you feel you are losing in your marriage, try a change in strategy. I have often heard it said that the definition of insanity (in this case, we will say failing in marriage) is doing the same thing while expecting different results. Why not lay down your pride and make a change?

Ask God for a new and better way. Pray for the Holy Spirit to give you His strategy for success. Make a fresh commitment to your marriage and spouse. Begin to expect something different by enacting this new strategy. Put the past expectations and behaviors behind you and begin to see a better and brighter future. The Bible tells us that He, the Holy Spirit, is a very present help in times of need. Call on and cooperate with Him and watch things change.

Be the Right Person

It is easy to fall into the trap of expecting from others what you are unwilling to give or be. Marriage is best only when each person is giving their best. So many have dreams and expectations of who they will marry. For the woman, it is Mr. Tall, Dark, and Handsome. It is the man who is wealthy, motivated, and the perfect gentleman. For the man, it is Miss America, Susie Homemaker, and a successful CEO, all while attending to his every need and desire. However, let's get real! Have you looked in the mirror lately? If we are honest with ourselves, we most likely fall short in one or all these areas.

However, I have good news for you. The Bible says you are fearfully and wonderfully made, and God has a good hope and future for you. You must understand that marriage is not about finding or even being the perfect person but rather striving daily to be the right person. Being the right person in your marriage relationship and to your spouse is required of us. We should never require of someone else what we ourselves are not willing to give. Ask the Lord to show you ways to be a better you for your spouse instead of seeking ways to improve your mate. Self-introspection is always better than verbal and mental criticism toward others. Be better, do better, love better, and live better!

Choose to Love

Although we all enjoy and desire the "feeling" of love, we must remember that, first and foremost, love is a verb and demands action. Begin to express your love, and the feelings will follow. Too many times, we equate love with what makes us feel all mushy-gushy inside, goose bumps up our spine, or butterflies in our belly. However, love is not a feeling.

Jesus loved in action by laying down His life for us. Likewise, husbands are commanded to love their wives as Christ loved the church and gave Himself for it. Wives are instructed to give themselves to their husbands. These descriptions are what love looks like. Feelings are real, but feelings are fleeting. Marriages will not succeed if they are based on the emotions of the moment. Successful relationships are the result of a decision to love regardless of feelings and the ***sheer commitment*** to make the choice to love in all seasons and all circumstances.

Celebrate Your Differences

Take a moment and rehearse the things that first caused you to be attracted to your spouse. Often, we allow the busyness of life to crowd in and cause us to forget all the little things that once made our spouse so attractive to us. We forget to celebrate our differences. Instead, we allow our differences to divide us rather than draw us together.

Remember, opposites attract! Magnets do not stick together because they possess the same polarity. As a matter of fact, one is called the north pole, and the other is the south pole. They are complete opposites.

Many times, we feel like we are from different worlds, and we let it divide us rather than draw us together. I am thankful that my husband does not possess the same personality and abilities that I do. He completes me, and I complete him. Together, we form the perfect balance. We form a complete picture—a perfect pair made in heaven. Celebrate your differences and depend on one another to assist in the places you may be insufficient. You need your spouse! God made it that way!

Becoming One Flesh

When we are married and pronounced husband and wife, it is the starting point. Although the Bible calls us one flesh, it is a process. We must allow the process to take place by giving grace and finding ways to agree rather than always demanding to be right or have things our way.

Robert and I came from similar backgrounds but were very different people with different thoughts on how things should and would be done. We had to learn to allow each other to express thoughts and ideas without always needing to be proven right because there are always different highways that lead to the same destination. Some may be more scenic, and some may get to the destination in a more timely manner; however, both achieve the same goal. Don't sweat the small stuff. Enjoy the ride, and celebrate the destination once you arrive. Life is a journey, so don't spend it quarreling with one another.

It is important that we allow the Holy Spirit to work in us to cause us to become one flesh. The most powerful force on earth is a husband and wife in agreement with each other. Allow yourself to become one flesh with your spouse and watch what the Lord will do in and through you.

Overcoming the Hurt

Along the road of life, we pick up habits and ways of doing things. We pack our suitcases with life experiences, and not all are worthy of preserving. If we fail to dispense of these hurtful encounters through forgiveness, we will hold ourselves captive to the past along with our relationships and marriage as well.

Life is good at dealing us with a card that is not always a winner, but with the Lord's help and allowing others to speak into our lives, we can be healed and create the dream marriage and life we desire. Forgiving those who have wronged us is key to moving forward in our families. Holding on to past hurt will cause bitterness to fester, which will harm our marital relationship and ultimately cause destruction. Do not allow yesterday's experiences to become the heavy baggage you carry for the rest of your life. Choose to forgive.

It's Not a One-Way Street

Many marriages fail because spouses take the attitude of "my way or the highway." Unfortunately, this thinking leads to just that—the highway of separation and divorce. Marriage is not a one-way street; we must learn to listen and prefer one another as a way of showing honor and respect to one another.

The apostle Paul said whatever we sow, we will also reap. Many reap the experience of not being heard or valued simply because they do not sow seeds of respect and honor. If we desire to be heard, we must first learn to listen.

Things within our marital relationship will not always be done our way or to our exact liking. Early in our relationship, my husband hated shopping but learned to tolerate it and appreciate being with me because he knew I enjoyed it. He was willing to sacrifice to see that I was happy. Likewise, I was willing to do things he liked, even if it was not my cup of tea. A lasting and fulfilling marriage is one where both parties are agreeable to setting aside their personal desires for each other's well-being and joy.

Friends Forever

Before you married, you were most likely friends and spent time together. You dated! Being married does not mean you should no longer do the same. It is essential to spend time together as friends, enjoying each other's company. Life gets so busy with our jobs, chores, children, and other things that we forget this simple concept: We should not merely be spouses and lovers; we should first be friends.

When we possess something that we value, we take care of it. Unfortunately, some people take better care of their car than they do their spouse. We seem to make time for things that are important to us. Your marriage is the most important thing, and value should be placed upon it. You do not have to spend mega-dollars every weekend or take dream vacations every year. Just stroll along the beach or in the park, curl up on the couch together, watch a movie with a bag of popcorn, or arrange a surprise lunch date. Whatever you choose, I assure you it is an investment worthy of the effort. You will be amazed at the payoff from this simple but significant investment.

You and your spouse should spend time together in order to stay connected on a personal and intimate level. Dating is an activity not merely for the unmarried but also for the married.

It is an opportunity to continue building open communication and relationships with one another. These relationship-building moments should not stop just because we live under the same roof. Don't stop dating; keep on being friends, and stop and smell the roses together.

Don't Compare

Social media, romance novels, movie stars, and other outlets will paint a picture of what you and your marriage should look like. However, this is simply not reality, and we are to never allow our expectations to be molded or formed by outside influences.

I do not love my husband because he is perfect and void of shortcomings. Likewise, I assure you that he does not love me because I am flawless. I love my husband because I made a commitment to love him in all circumstances and situations, and he did the same. We promised: "'til death do us part." Regardless of what you see or hear, there is no perfect person, relationship, or marriage. The Bible declares we are in the process of being transformed into the image of Christ, and I know of no one who has yet arrived; we are all a work in progress. So, be encouraged; there is still hope for you and your marriage.

Many spend too much time peering into other people's lives and forming unrealistic ideas and expectations based on what they see displayed. They know little about those they seek advice from regarding life and relationships. This conduct is extremely dangerous and detrimental to marriages.

What if we stopped spending time peering into the lives of others and instead focused on creating an environment that we desire to see in our marriage? What if we stopped comparing our marriages with the influencers and became an example for others to follow? If you put as much time and effort into your relationship as you fantasize about someone else's, you could have the marriage of your dreams. It is vital to your relationship that you do not fall into the trap of comparison. The Bible says that those who compare themselves with others are unwise. This is not the category in which I desire for my life or marriage to be placed.

You and your spouse are each unique, and God has a great plan and purpose for you personally and as a couple. Begin to seek Him! True fulfillment will only come as you walk in the fullness of what He has planned for you. No Hollywood movie, Instagram® influencers, or romance novel could ever compare to the story God has written for you to live and experience together.

Transparency

To have a marriage that will stand the test of time, you must have complete and utter transparency and honesty. There can be no secret activity or behavior within the relationship. When secrets are kept from one another, trust cannot be built.

We must share everything with our spouse so trust can be built into the very fabric of our relationship. This is how we construct a house that will stand and be a testimony of the goodness and grace of God to others. Storms may come, but your home will stand because you are totally open and honest; you keep nothing hidden because you are truly, as the Bible says, one flesh.

In our home, nothing is off-limits. We share passwords, phones, iPads®, thoughts, opinions, etc. There is nothing to hide from one another. Why would I not share everything with the person who I love and loves me? Why would I withhold from someone I trust and who trusts me completely? Transparency is the way a marriage is designed to be.

When we withhold things from one another, it becomes an open door for the enemy to get a foothold in our marriage, breaking trust and eventually injuring the relationship. However, if we are open and honest, withholding nothing from one another, we will have a marriage that can stand the test of time and any storm or anything the enemy may attempt to throw our way. You have greater power over the enemy when you are unified and on the same page. The way to become one flesh is through total and complete honesty and transparency.

The Bible says freedom comes when operating in truth. Freedom is always better than the agony of bondage. Secrets will not produce a healthy relationship or a godly way to live. Truth and transparency are the only ways to have a healthy and heaven-blessed marriage.

Say No to Divorce

Today, many think divorce is the easy way out. However, it leaves behind hurt, brokenness, mistrust, and many other wounds that must later be healed to move forward in life. Divorce is not the solution to fixing your life. Often, we are guilty of letting the enemy trick us into thinking that if we just had our freedom, our lives would be better. The thought is, "*If I didn't have to deal with this person I married, all problems would cease.*" However, that is just the enemy's ploy to conquer and divide your marriage.

We must remove divorce from our conversations. Sometimes, it is used as a weapon to control certain situations and circumstances. This attitude is nothing other than manipulation and is harmful to the relationship. We should never issue threats of separation or divorce; instead, remove it entirely from your marital vocabulary.

Just because you presently have an imperfect marriage does not mean it cannot be healed if you allow the Lord to do a work in it. I have known people who thought divorce was the answer to all their marital problems and if they had a different spouse, things would be different. I watched as they made the unfortunate decision to divorce and "move on." I witnessed them struggling with the same matters throughout their lives due to unresolved issues. You must deal with the issues in your own heart and mind, or you will continue on the merry-go-round of broken relationships.

A Work in Progress

You see, there are no perfect people, including you and me. We are all a work in progress being conformed to the image of Christ. Your marriage is made up of two imperfect people. Unfortunately, the expectations for our spouse are greater than what we require of ourselves, thus leading to constant frustration and fault-finding. What if you stop picking your spouse apart and start praying for them? Instead, what if you ask the Lord to change and conform yourself to His image and likeness? If we were half as nice to our spouse as others, we would have far fewer issues in our marriage. Sometimes, we just need to show love and be joyful. Learn to be patient and show kindness with a gentle spirit. This will make a huge difference in your life.

I encourage you to remove the word "divorce" and replace it with words of intercession for your spouse, words that will build your relationship. Speak words that will promote love and unity instead of hurt and uncertainty, which is the language of the enemy that divides. Refuse to be his mouthpiece to destroy your marriage and home.

In extreme situations, there are times when a spouse has gone too far, and divorce is the only option. There is no condemnation to anyone who has gone through a divorce, particularly when it is biblically justified, and all remedies have been exhausted. However, I have seen with my own eyes God healing broken marriages and restoring love that was lost. So, if you are in a place of hopelessness, remember: Jesus saves, Jesus heals, and Jesus delivers! Nothing is impossible for Him.

Show a Little Kindness

Not only do we need to remove the words "divorce" and "separation" from our vocabulary, but also words and communications that do nothing but stir strife and division. Remember, the Bible tells us that death and life are in the power of the tongue, and you will eat its fruit. What are you chewing on? Is it constant strife and anger? Is it disgust and hatred? Is it hurt and disappointment? If so, try changing your vocabulary to speak words that bring life to your situation.

Perhaps you say, "*It's not me, it's them.*" Maybe they are the culprit. However, the Bible also declares that a soft answer turns away wrath (Proverbs 15:1). Do not respond to angry words or actions with the same. Try taking the high road and offer words of love and kindness. Choose to speak words of love and appreciation as you pray that God will work in your home and marriage.

Often, we want to speak and defend rather than listen and contemplate before responding. I have been guilty many times of this type of behavior. It takes great discipline to listen instead of react. However, it is always better to listen than to be heard. The Bible commands us to be quick to hear and slow to speak. In obeying this command, you will find that your conversations will be much less stressful and more productive. This is a trait that we all should possess. Ask for help from the Holy Spirit to hold your tongue and give you ears to hear what your spouse is expressing. Put down your dukes and give place to hear clearly before you respond.

Growing Together

Our marital relationship should be constantly growing. It should grow in communication, love, intimacy, and friendship. It is much like a garden; the more you tend to it, the more fruit you will have. It is important to give time to the garden of your marriage.

Unfortunately, many marriages grow apart rather than grow stronger together. They allow the weeds of life to take over and become wrapped up in everything but each other. Men seem to need their hunting, fishing, car racing, golfing trips, or nights out with the guys. Women want their spa dates, shopping trips, girls' weekends, and concerts. While nothing is inherently wrong with many of these things, they can rob you of time that could be spent with your spouse. Many people have fallen into this trap and spend more time apart than they do together. This should not happen because an unattended garden will not grow and flourish; it will eventually die.

We must make time for each other. The truth is that you are better together! You need to take time to water your garden and pull the weeds that your lack of attention has allowed in the precious space of your relationship. Set aside time to spend together instead of apart.

It is crucial to recognize that the grass is not greener on the other side. You can have the most beautiful lawn (marriage) on the block; it just takes time and effort. Your marriage is worth it.

No one and nothing should ever take precedence over your spouse and marriage. Put each other first and watch God restore everything you have desired. Watch your marriage blossom as the fruit of your labor and time produce the fruits of unity, love, and friendship. Remember, life is a journey, not a race. Enjoy life together, and stop and smell the roses.

Let It Burn

With the busyness of life, we forget that one of the most significant ways to be unified with our spouse is to give ourselves sexually. As the Bible commands, we are not to withhold ourselves from our spouses. God created us to be sexually active with the one person to whom we said, "I do." Sex is something beautiful that God created and ordained to be experienced and enjoyed between one man and one woman within the contract of marriage.

It is good when a man and woman come together to pleasure one another. Some have said that sex is the finest form of spiritual warfare a couple can do together because of the total and complete unity that happens in that moment. There is a closeness felt that can be experienced in no other way.

When God created man and woman, he told them to be fruitful and multiply. Sexual intercourse is the only way for that to happen. So, God not only commanded us to have sex with our spouse, but he also placed within both man and woman the desire for sexual union.

When God created man and woman, He did not create nor offer any other suggestions as to what they needed other than each other. You do not need objects, toys, people, videos, or pictures to have a healthy sex life. You are enough for your spouse, and they are enough for you. God made it that way. It is beautiful what God did at creation, and we should agree with Him.

And They Lived…

Marriage is comprised of two people, one man and one woman. Specifically, it is made up of you and your spouse. Together, you make the greatest team God ever created. You can have heaven on earth when you are united and put Him first in every area of your relationship, whether communication, decisions, time, intimacy, or children. The fairy tale marriage you dreamed of once upon a time can become a reality. And then, the story of your marriage can end with these words… AND THEY LIVED HAPPILY EVER AFTER!

More Than Just Words

Sheer commitment is not merely the answer to a question my husband was asked over a decade ago—neither is it just a book title—nor a catchy phrase used throughout this writing. *Sheer commitment* is a way of life. It is the road to seeing a successful, thriving marriage. Let this be more than a book you read; let it be a motto by which you live!

About the Author

STACEY GAY is a devoted wife, mother, grandmother, and pastor with a heart for empowering families. She has been married to her husband, Robert, for over 40 years. Together, they have built a legacy of faith with their three children, who serve in ministry alongside their spouses, and nine cherished grandchildren. Stacey and Robert are the founding pastors of High Praise Worship Center International in Panama City, Florida. Since planting the church in 1997, they have witnessed its growth into a thriving ministry that now oversees multiple churches and ministers under their apostolic leadership. With a vision to equip believers for strong and resilient marriages and families, Stacey is passionate about seeing individuals walk in God's purpose for their lives. Her ministry continues to inspire and strengthen countless lives across generations.

HIGH
PRAISE
PANAMA CITY
HIGHPRAISE.CHURCH
Pastors
JOSHUA &
MIRANDA
GAY
SCAN FOR
MORE INFO
HIGH
PRAISE
CRESTVIEW
HIGHPRAISECRESTVIEW.COM
Pastors
MICAH &
CHELSEA
GAY
SCAN FOR
MORE INFO

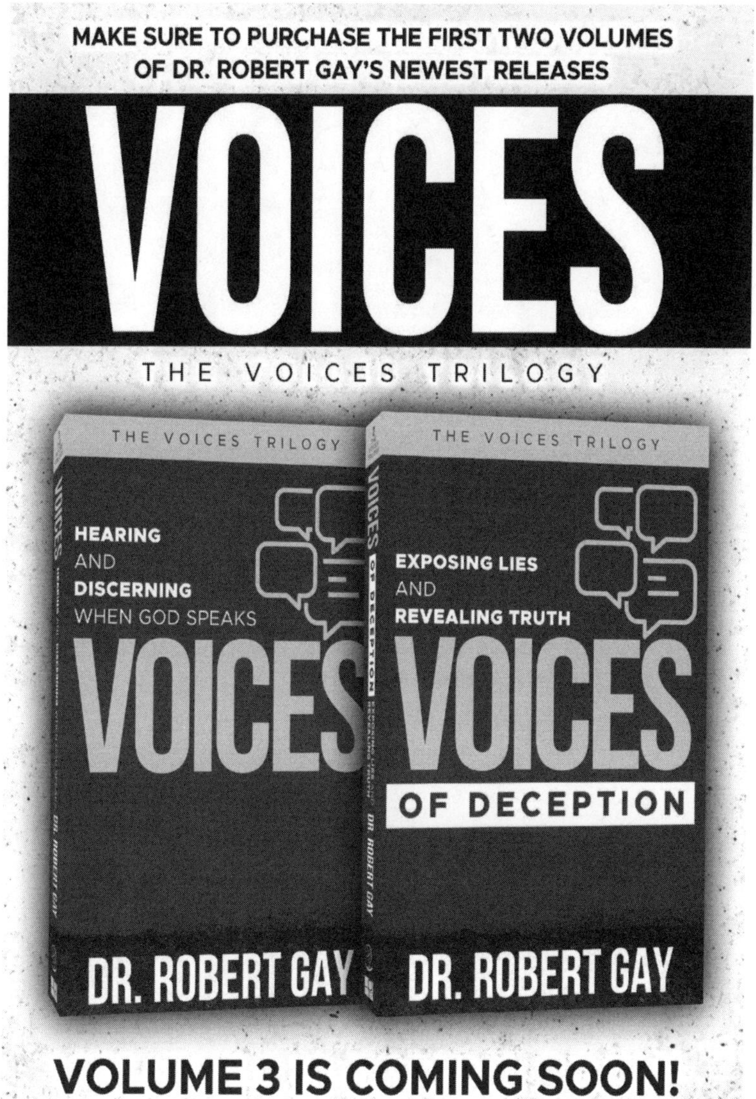
MAKE SURE TO PURCHASE THE FIRST TWO VOLUMES
OF DR. ROBERT GAY'S NEWEST RELEASES
VOICES
THE VOICES TRILOGY
THE VOICES TRILOGY
HEARING
AND
DISCERNING
WHEN GOD SPEAKS
VOICES
DR. ROBERT GAY
THE VOICES TRILOGY
EXPOSING LIES
AND
REVEALING TRUTH
VOICES
OF DECEPTION
DR. ROBERT GAY
VOLUME 3 IS COMING SOON!

Jesus In 3D
Pastor Robert Gay

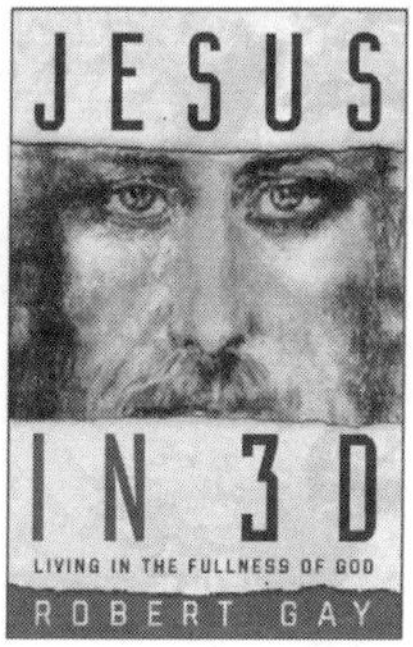

Do you want to express the life of God in every aspect of your life? In your ministry? For us to walk in the totality of Jesus, we must first cherish the fullness of His ministry. Every dimension of the ministry of Jesus is critical for us to have ultimate effectiveness for the kingdom of God. Today, if you want to reflect the life of God, you must receive and activate all that He did, everything He said, and everything He demonstrated.

Revolutionaires
Pastor Joshua Gay

Revolutionaries declares to readers that God is raising up a transformation generation in the earth today. Discover the life of a spiritual revolutionary through the study of scripture and parallels from history.

"...if you read this book you are going to be enlightened, motivated and activated into being one of God's "Revolutionaries." - Dr. Bill Hamon

Building Strong
Pastor Robert Gay

There is a blueprint that the Father has rendered for the design of the Church. Jesus has been given the responsibility of building what was in the mind of the Father from creation. The Holy Spirit is the agent that empowers and gifts the spiritual subcontractors here on earth to build according to the plan that has been rendered from heaven.

HIGH PRAISE MEDIA PRODUCTS for more products or to order any of these products visit our online store at
WWW.HIGHPRAISEPC.COM/ONLINE-STORE

GET THE NEW WORSHIP ALBUM FROM
HIGH PRAISE WORSHIP
GOD
OF THE
TURNAROUND
HIGH PRAISE WORSHIP
ORDER CD COPY BY CALLING (850) 874-9745
OR STREAM AND DOWNLOAD FROM
YOUR FAVORITE MUSIC PLATFORM
Available on iTunes
Listen On Spotify
available on amazonmusic